"There will always be those times in our lives when what we need most is the comfort of knowing 'It will be alright' . . . and those days when the tinniest spark of hope can pull us through the inferno of pain, doubt and confusion. For those in need of compassion's touch and proof that you can begin anew . . . this book is a must"

—Willie Aames, Actor/Author

"Unwavering Strength is true to its word: it will give you just that. This moving book is full of stories that will uplift you, support you, guide you and comfort you. It is a book long overdue about the possibilities of choice and perspective in dealing with cancer, and yet it applies to all overwhelming challenges. Read it. It will give you power."

—Dee Wallace, Healer, Author and Actress

"These stories are gems of faith, and can help anyone feel better when going through a rough time. The writers are gifted and share much needed uplifting stories. This book is a must read!"

—Bob Proctor, Best-Selling Author, *You Were Born Rich* and the star of *The Secret*

"When life overwhelms you and you feel a bit defeated, pick up this book. In Unwavering Strength, the authors take you on a journey that will help you heal your heart so that you can live a happy and joyful life."

—Marci Shimoff, Professional Speaker, #1 NY Times Bestselling Author, *Happy for No Reason, Love For No Reason, Chicken Soup for the Woman's Soul*

"The writers of this book have experienced profound grief. They hope their hard-won wisdom can light the way for others."

—George Meyer, Producer and writer for *The Simpsons,* and formerly *Saturday Night Live*

"This is a wonderful inspirational book that will show you that you too can overcome challenges in your life. The authors share with you great advice on how to stay positive and find a way back to peace and happiness. I highly recommend this book."

—Arielle Ford, Author, *The Secret Soulmate*

"Excellent book on reminding you that you are strong enough to get through the rough times and that no matter where you are in life, help comes in mysterious ways. Judy O'Beirn is amazing and the book is one to keep close to you for years."

—Mary Morrissey, International Speaker, BestSelling Author, CEO Consultant, Visionary, Empowerment Specialist

"This book is an easy read with its many short stories. It works for every one including busy people who may only be able to read a few pages at a sitting. The message in the stories always leave me feeling good!"

—Judith Orloff, MD, International Bestselling Author, *The Ecstasy of Surrender*

"I appreciate that each of the authors in this book opened their heart and shared their struggles. And what I like the best is that it did not beat them, it gave them the strength to rise above and find the best in what life has to offer. We all experience contrast, and the important distinction is what we do with it."

—Christy Whitman, New York Times Bestselling Author

"Life is not about what happens to you, rather it's about how you respond. This book shows you that you too can face and embrace the stress of life and like coal under pressure, come out a shiny diamond. I love this book!"

—Dr. Darren R. Weissman, Developer of the Lifeline Technique

"Life is a never-ending series of adventures that take us to the deepest parts. . . and expand us the most through the toughest times. If you're ready to feel like you're not alone and even find some reprieve from the lower moments in life, this book does the trick. Be ready to feel renewed, inspired and for a sense of new possibilities open up. You're in good hands with Judy's remarkable wisdom."

—Jennifer McLean, Host *Healing With The Masters*, Creator, *Living Your Success Signature Business*

"During these challenging times, the question is, where do I turn for answers? This book if full of amazing stories by real people, like you and me, that got through it and became "victors" rather than "victims". It is a must read and one that I will sending all my friends and family."

—Dr. Fabrizio Mancini, Bestselling Author, *The Power of Self-Healing* http://drfabmancini.com

"Unwavering Strength features empowering stories of strength, courage and perseverance and will inspire you to believe that even in the darkest days there is always hope. These stories show just how unquenchable the human spirit is and how strong we really are when we need to be."

—Linda Joy, Bestselling Publisher & Inspirational Catalyst www.InspiredLivingPublishing.com

"Unwavering Strength is a must-read for everyone who wants to be inspiried in a challenging world in which inspiration is much-needed. Thank you to Judy O'Beirn for bringing together an amazing group of authors who are pillars of strength and true Ambassadors."

—Natalie Ledwell, Bestselling Author & co-founder of Mind Movies

"The stories are uplifting and filled with hope on subjects that would otherwise make you think there is no hope or very little hope. I am in awe of all who shared their story with us. Everyone needs to read this book, it's for anyone who has ever cared for another human being *afflicted with any type of illness or affected by trauma because sooner or later every one of us will face this in his or her life."*

—Rick Frishman Bestselling Author, Publisher & Speaker

"Do yourself a soulfully-inspired favor and buy this book to uplift you during your most challenging times. Then, do your loved ones a favor, and buy it for them, as well. They will love you for it. Anyone who reads this book will undoubtedly walk away feeling stronger, more courageous and capable of rising above any obstacle that comes their way."

—Cari L. Murphy, Soul Success Coach, Award Winning Media Host, International Bestselling Author

"People who can capture your heart through courage and inner strength built from overcoming challenges are a true inspiration. Each story in Unwavering Strength does just that. I recommend you read this book that takes you on a healing journey you will never forget."

—Debra Oakland, Living In Courage Online
http://www.livingincourageonline.com

"This book will teach you that you have the light, the strength and the courage within to get through an adversity life challenges you with. You are more powerful than you know and this book will confirm that!

—Tara Taylor Intuitive Counselor, Author and Advocate of Love!
www.tarataylor.ca

"If you ever looked for a book of stories to inspire you and others, this is the book to buy. Each precious story inspires and engages you in a life topic, like bullying, faith, and letting go. Each author captivates you in their own journey and gives you the tools to overcome."

 —Lisa Mininni Best Selling Author, *Me, Myself, and Why? The Secrets to Navigating Change,* President, ExcellerateAssociates.com

"Inspiring. Uplifting. Writers from all over the world sharing their stories of what got them through their challenging times. Makes a great gift for others or for yourself."

—Sunny Dawn Johnston, International Speaker, Bestselling Author and Psychic Medium

"Unwavering Strength is filled with wonderful stories of courage, triumph and love. It shows just how unquenchable the human spirit is and how strong we really are when we need to be. It's hugely moving and uplifting."

—Keith Leon, Multiple Bestselling Author, Publisher & Book Mentor
www.BabypiePublishing.com

"Unwavering Strength is an absolutely inspiring read! I so enjoyed going on the journey of each author's story, and found myself identifying with many of them. If you are feeling stuck or lost or uninspired, this book will lift you right out of that and into the light of hope and healing.

—Dina Proctor, best-selling author, *Madly Chasing Peace: How I Went from Hell to Happy in Nine Minutes a Day*,
www.madlychasingpeace.com

"This is so much more than a book! If you feel like you're facing a maintain that you just can't climb, this book is your life-line! Within its pages you'll discover the secrets to finding strength, resolve, hope and measures of love you never knew existed. There are many stories in this book; one of them is yours. Find it, read it and use it to draw from within yourself the strength you already have to climb that mountain; whatever it is. It's unwavering strength; and you'll find it in these pages."

—Steve Lowell, International Speaker & Professional Speaking Mentor

"Although I've read many stories in my life of people overcoming great adversity, I've never read a book where all the stories, as painful as they are, touched me so deeply and also left me feeling inspired and uplifted. Where did Judy find these amazing people—each one of whom suffered an unimaginable loss and yet turned their loss into a contribution to our world? Reading just one of these author's contributions to this powerful book will change your life forever."

—Debra Poneman, Best-selling Author and Founder of Yes to Success Seminars, Inc.

"Unwavering Strength is a must-read for everyone who wants to be inspired in a challenging world in which inspiration is much-needed. Thank you to Judy O'Beirn for bringing together an amazing group of authors who are pillars of strength and true Ambassadors."

—Lisa Larter, Founder of The Pilot Project and Social Media Expert

"_Unwavering Strength_ is chock full of wonderful stories of strength, courage and the triumph of love. It shows just how unquenchable the human spirit is and how strong we really are when we need to be."

—Eva Gregory, Author, _The Feel Good Guide To Prosperity_

"Sometimes life delivers the unexpected and it can feel like a never ending spiral downward (I've been there, done that!). This book will help you pick yourself up and live life more fully! "

—Jeanna Gabellini, Author, _10-Minute Money Makers_

Unwavering Strength

Judy O'Beirn
& friends

Cover Design
Killer Covers

www.KillerCovers.com

Layout
Ginger Marks
DocUmeant Designs

www.DocUmeantDesigns.com

ISBN-13: 978-1500894986 (CreateSpace-Assigned)
ISBN-10: 1500894982

This book is dedicated to my husband, Gerry O'Beirn who showed *Unwavering Strength* as he sat holding hands with his sisters, and my mother, as they went through their own battle with cancer. In three-and-a-half short years we lost Gerry's sisters Evelyn Mills and Marlene Long, my Mom, Rita McColl, my daughters' best friend Carrie Ough, our dog Snickers, and Gerry himself.

Here is to our G.E.M.s whom you will meet in the pages of this book—who taught each of us to have *Unwavering Strength*.

This poem was written as a dedication to our G.E.M.s

by Jennifer Gibson

Although you cannot see me
I'm never far away
And while I know you'll miss me
Please know that I'm okay
Remember all the good times
The laughter through the years
Celebrate my life
Wipe away your tears
Love me, miss me, but let me go
For I've finally been set free
I'm now soaring like an eagle
Towards a new destiny
No matter where life takes you
By your side I'll be
To hold your hand & give you strength
Just as you did for me
So although we're not together
We're never far apart
For every time you think of me
I'll be there in your heart.

Recorded and sung by Kristen Sharma

Contents

Acknowledgments

Thank you to the following individuals who without their contributions and support this book would not have been written.

First, thank you to my late husband, Gerry, who continues to inspire me daily to live life to its fullest and cherish the people in my life. I feel his love around me still and I will forever be grateful for the time I was blessed to have with him. I thank my mother and father, Rita and Bob, for making me who I am today and I miss them every day.

Thank you to my sister, Peggy McColl, for being my pillar of strength through the years and for always being here for me. Her contribution to my book (the Foreword) is so very appreciated along with lending me her ear and her expertise during this project.

I would like to express my gratitude to the many people who saw me through this book; to all those who provided support, talked things over, read, wrote, offered comments, allowed me to quote their remarks and assisted in the editing, proofreading and design.

Jenn Gibson, my daughter, should probably have her name as one of the authors. She has worked tirelessly with me to pull together the book and the stories and all the promotion and events.

My daughter Amy Lusk who unselfishly gave her best friend Carrie unwavering strength. And my step kids Katie O'Beirn and Nick O'Beirn, who have been with me throughout this journey and whose Dad would be very proud of them for the wonderful adults our kids have become.

I would like to thank Tami King and Phil Marks for helping me in the extensive process of editing. Tami spent countless hours reading the stories and giving feedback, and rewriting and mentoring authors to bring their amazing stories to the pages of this book. Phil was going through a difficult time with a friend of his and yet he didn't hesitate to help with whatever was needed of him. Thank you to Ginger Marks your enthusiasm is contagious and creativity is wonderful. You made this part of the process fun; Krystle Worster for helping with the set up and e-book conversion; Casey Demchak and Al Henderson for their superb copy writing skills; and to Colin Miller for his unlimited time spent on the Unwavering Strength website.

Thank you to Sandy Alemian for doing Podcasts with all of the co-authors and to Anya Sophia Mann for taking the time to interview every co-author on her radio show, Unwavering Strength Radio.

Throughout the process of writing this book, many individuals have taken time out to help me that I would like to thank. Just a few are Emmanuel Dagher, Bill King and Deb Scott.

Sandy Alemian and Tara Taylor thank you from the bottom of my heart. I have no idea where I would be without you two talking and talking and talking with me for countless hours to help me with my grief. I will be forever grateful for your unwavering support.

Rhonda Mills, my niece, and Amy Lusk who have been working alongside me to pull together our annual GEM Golf tournament which raises money for families going through cancer.

To my new friends in Florida, Kathy & Jeff Bull, Becky & Neil Levesque, and Amy & Paul Williams, you have been instrumental in changing my life and reminding me to live every moment to it's fullest.

Thanks to all my friends for sharing my happiness when starting this project and following with encouragement when it seemed too difficult to be completed.

I am truly honored by the gift of music and songs created as a companion to this book. Kristen Sharma, Jennifer Gibson, Joe Merrick, Irit and Ishay Oz created three beautiful and unique versions of Unwavering Strength. I am forever grateful for this gift. Listen to them with an open heart and let them heal you.

Last and certainly not least: I would like to thank each and every wonderful co-author. Without their inspiring contributions, this book would not have been possible.

Foreword

I had a front row seat to watch the challenges that my sister Judy, the creator of this book and contributing author, went through. This is not the kind of a front row that people line up early for. It was difficult for me, it was difficult for those involved and it was extremely difficult for her.

It was hard to imagine that one person would be challenged with so many sequential and emotionally painful experiences as Judy did. After all, everyone goes through challenges. . . but this many, one after another!

Ultimately, Judy's experience birthed the idea behind something far bigger than her, or any of the people you are about to read about. Unwavering Strength are true stories of individuals who have endured tremendous challenges.

In this book you will discover true authentic courage. A variety of strong individuals have come forth to share their darkest times designed to bring light to others.

I see this book as a delicious smorgasbord of delightful snacks. You can choose to eat all of them (as they are all easily digestible) or, if you have an eager appetite sit down and devour it all in one sitting. Either way, it is totally fulfilling.

In this book you will hear from Annie who claims:

"We must accept the duality of life: good and bad, right and wrong, up and down, sadness and joy, loss and life. The key is making the choice to find the good within the maze of confusion."

Willie will show you what GRITT really stands for.

And Silke will invite you to never take freedom for granted.

And Evelyn who brilliantly shared: "Life is somewhat like a blueberry muffin. We can focus on the squished berries, the lopsided muffin top, and the crumbs—or we can savor the overall sweetness and delight."

John proclaims: "From the happiest of the circumstance to the darkest, each served a purpose."

Is it possible that *Unwavering Strength* is to serve a purpose in your life?

I believe it can. It is my highest recommendation that you invest some quality time with this book of collective stories of true unwavering strength. Share the book and the stories with others and be sure to gift someone you care about with their own copy as well.

When we help another, in any way, whether it is a gift of advice, a morsel of strength or with sharing a copy of Unwavering Strength, you are giving out good. Good will always come back to you.

—Peggy McColl
New York Times Best-Selling Author aka "The Best Seller Maker"
http://peggymccoll.com/

Introduction

He was a handsome fellow with salt-and-pepper hair and I'd known him for about a decade before I received the phone call that would change my life forever. Gerry O'Beirn was a quiet man but after so many years of being neighbors, I actually began to take notice of him. And I liked what I saw—a lot. I knew he had kids and I'd heard he was going through a divorce so when he called one day to ask if my mother and I would like to take in a border—him! —I was definitely open to the possibility. And let's face it, what woman wouldn't want to have a good-looking guy around the house?!

Once he had been staying with me awhile, I realized fairly quickly that Gerry and I were falling in love. We had so much in common, including the experience of having lost a sibling in adulthood, which made us appreciate how precious life was. We did our best to enjoy every moment—to laugh at the little things that might otherwise annoy us, and we valued the time spent with our family and friends.

Our mutual love of travel inspired us to hop in the car for road trips all over the United States and Canada. We travelled to Nashville, San Francisco, San Diego, Nova Scotia, Prince Edward Island, Florida, Missouri, New York City and our feelings for each other grew stronger with each destination we explored.

When Gerry and I decided to get married, we chose to have a destination wedding. Our families were excited for both of us and looked forward to coming together on a beach in Hawaii. The only damper in our wedding plans was that my mother wasn't feeling well and I knew her physical discomfort had to be serious if she was backing out of the trip because she thought Gerry was terrific and she was incredibly happy for the two us. Mom promised to check with the doctor and get some tests run while we were gone and we all did our best not to worry about her mysterious ailment. My wedding turned out beautifully and we cruised around the islands, splashed about in the waves, toasted with champagne, and looked forward to our life together as a blended family.

That was the beginning of a sequence of events that would completely alter the course of my life. It inspired me to write this book and dedicate myself to helping families affected by cancer. I have learned more than I ever thought I would know about this disease and the many forms it takes. I learned that it operates on its own schedule. As much as the doctors want to help you have some predictability in your life, you can't know for sure how quickly it will grow in the body, or how a person will respond to treatments, or whether the side effects of the chemotherapy and radiation will be as devastating as the disease.

I didn't know how strong I was until cancer struck my family and I had to say good-bye to far too many people far too soon. I am still reeling from my losses but the one thing that propels me out of bed on the worst mornings, when my grief threatens to make my limbs as heavy as lead and my heart aches so much that I can't stand it, is knowing that I can use this experience to help others. "Judy," I tell myself, "you've got important work to do. So move it!"

One memory I repeatedly have is watching Gerry with one family member after another as they succumbed to cancer; he possessed this unwavering strength as he held their hands while they waited for news, recovered from surgery, and struggled to maintain their morale. That's what I wish for everyone dealing with the devastation of cancer and it's why I've titled this book Unwavering Strength. I believe there will be moments when you feel that your challenges are just too much, but if you look around, you will see others who want to help you shoulder your burdens and give you respite and comfort so you can come back with the courage, faith, and stamina you need. There is so much to learn from others who have already walked this road. This is the book I wish I'd had when I was helping my family, because of the stories and because of the incredible authors that share their amazing journeys to inspire us to renew hope and to know we are not alone.

Gerry's unwavering strength helped me to believe that I, too, could be strong. I could not have gotten through the worst of this experience of losing loved ones if it hadn't been for his example and support. That's why I felt compelled to put together this book and share with you my story and the stories of others who have gone through their own challenging time and been there with family members and friends to help them. It is a book for anyone that has experienced devastation, loss, trauma or death. All the people who wrote a piece for this book have been willing to open their hearts and reveal their vulnerabilities, and I'm very grateful to every one of them.

I am especially thankful to my friends and family members who have encouraged me to create this book. I am deeply grateful that Debbie Ford had generously offered to write the foreword and it is with a heavy heart that I tell you she passed away last year before she had the chance. Her book Courage, about her battle with cancer, inspires us to believe that we, too, can be brave. I offer a very special thank you to my sister, Peggy McColl, who wrote the foreword and who has been a pillar of strength for our family and me.

Cancer doesn't happen in a vacuum. Everyone around the cancer patient is affected by it. Everyone feels the uncertainty, the hopelessness, and the fear. Everyone has to adjust their lives around a new, uneven rhythm of time spent in hospitals, ERs, doctor's offices, and clinics. Routines disappear like your waistline as you age. Until your stomach rumbles, you can easily forget that it's long past dinnertime. Your mind swirls when trying to decide whether to stay with your loved one; to hold their frail hand with a grip weakened by yet another surgery; or go to work and see if you can get something done to try to catch up. There comes a point where deciding whether to have the cook in the hospital cafeteria scramble or fry your eggs completely stumps you, but you somehow carry on despite your weariness.

Whether you are the spouse, partner, child, parent, best friend, cousin, or neighbor, it's easy to underestimate how much another person's cancer will affect you. Caretaking takes its toll physically and emotionally—and mentally too, which you'll realize as you stammer in response to, "Ma'am? Scrambled or friend?" Huh?

Health issues take their toll financially as well. Your loved one can have the very best health insurance available but it won't pay for everything. You may have to open your wallet or checkbook to cover meals on the go, hotel stays near the clinic far from your home, or day care and babysitting for your young children who used to be cared for by your now-sick spouse. Experimental treatments that could save your loved ones life are rarely covered. As you become more tired, less focused, and less productive at work, you start to worry about your job, and maybe you even jeopardize your position or lose clients. You don't think about the money when you are fighting for someone's life, but the bills can pile up rapidly, adding to the stress and uncertainty.

That's why I am donating a percentage of the proceeds from this book to helping other families in crisis who are struggling with all the aspects of helping a loved one with cancer. There are so many situations that we just don't think about until we're in them. We never know where cancer will strike or when. When we hear the diagnosis, we feel blindsided. Our natural inclination is to ask, "What can I do?" The patient and their family and friends aren't quite sure how to answer that at first because this is such new territory. They may be embarrassed to accept help but we should continue to ask—and to be creative in finding ways to assist. We can ask others who have been in the situation, "What do you think I could offer to do for this person and family I care so much about?" I hope this book will give you some ideas through its sharing of stories about how people have coped with having cancer or having a loved one suffer from it. Even if you can only bring someone a healthy lunch to keep them going as they keep a bedside vigil, to listen to them with love and acceptance when they are expressing their fears, or call them in the lonely weeks after a funeral to let them know you are thinking about them, you CAN make a difference. I am not sure how we will beat cancer. What I do know is that each of us has the power to rob it of much of its power by reaching out, in love and community, to those who are suffering.

When I began this book, I thought it would be solely about cancer but thanks to a truly amazing group of Ambassadors of Strength, it has blossomed into a book about courage, strength and the power of love. The stories in this book have been shared in the hopes of inspiring you to find strength and comfort within these pages. From illness, tragedy, and loss to phobias, daring escapes, and bullying, these stories are about vastly different experiences but are all similar in their message. The strength and power to overcome all types of adversity lies within each one of us—but we are not alone. Let U.S. do it together.

The Epitome of Unwavering Strength

Judy O'Beirn

"I have found that if you love life, life will love you back."
—Arthur Rubinstein

As my family stood on the sparkling Maui beach with Gerry and I, the two of us said our vows. We kissed as the waves crashed against the rocks in the background and then began our celebration, enjoying this magical destination wedding and vacation with our now-blended family. What a beautiful day in one of the most beautiful places on earth. We were on top of the world and we were so very fortunate to have found each other. Life was a gift.

Unfortunately, my mother couldn't be there to share it with us. Gerry and I had been so disappointed when she made the decision not to come along. She had been fatigued a lot recently, and was losing weight. "I just don't feel well enough to make the trip," she said apologetically. "And besides Snickers needs someone to care for him. I'll take care of the house, so go enjoy yourselves and we will celebrate when you return."

We thought it could be something serious for her to miss out on such a big family event. Still, we did our best to be optimistic. The doctors would have some answers for her soon.

Just a few short months later, my mom would be diagnosed with Stage IV lung cancer. For all of us to go from such joy to such sadness was a shock.

We McColls had become more familiar with caretaking for loved ones with cancer than most people would ever want to be. We had lost our brother, Gary, to cancer a few years previously, and my dad, who died of a stroke in 2005, had battled the disease as well. Mom's prognosis was not good, but we weren't willing to give up hope. My brother, sister, Gerry, and I, along with our respective families, had started to accept what was going on. We gathered our forces and began the long vigil by her side, taking care of her, making her laugh, keeping her living her life.

My sister, Peggy, offered to take mom on a trip to Florida where she could spend time in one of her favorite places with friends she loved. Every holiday vacation we spent as a family laughing, eating, taking pictures, and enjoying our time together. One of the most difficult decisions she made was to buy each grandchild a very special necklace. With each birthday the tears poured but our hearts knew that we had a lasting symbol of her love.

In August of 2008, mom had a heart attack. We had no idea if she would survive the day never mind the next few months. Little did the doctors know she had an amazing will to live. We all spent every hour with her, and I know it helped her to have family with her at this time. As the weeks passed, we came to realize that keeping a calendar would allow one of us to be with Mom every day so the other family members could get some rest. If all of us were there all the time, it would be way too much to handle.

One of the first lessons of dealing with cancer is that it's a marathon, not a sprint. There comes a point where another cup of coffee isn't going to be enough to fuel you, and you have to get a break and rest. The emotional toll it takes really puts a strain on your body as well as your mood. It's hard to be strong and cheery when you're feeling more and more worn out.

I had grown especially close to mom after dad passed away. It had been just the two of us and her dog, Heidi, living in our house when Gerry, a handsome fellow who lived about ten minutes away, called to ask if she and I wanted to take in a border. When he told us that he was the border he had in mind, I was surprised, happy, and intrigued. I thought he was very attractive and wanted to get to know him better, so the plan sounded good to me!

Mom agreed, Gerry moved in, the three of us got along wonderfully, and very soon, Gerry and I fell in love. Lucky for us, his family enjoyed mine and vice versa, so everyone was very excited and thrilled when we announced we were going to marry.

When Gerry and I came home from our honeymoon we were faced with a new normal—driving Mom to doctors' appointments, checking in to see how she was feeling, making dinners, arranging constant care, and logging many hours by her bedside as her condition deteriorated. We were emotionally adjusting to what was happening, but it still felt far too soon to say good-bye when she passed away in October, almost a year to the day after Gerry and I said our vows.

As hard as it was to process my grief, I knew I had to keep going. I worked in the auto industry and had just begun to help my sister, Peggy McColl, part-time, assisting her with book marketing campaigns. I enjoyed the work, but I was focused on my day job which, to be honest, I had neglected a bit while caring for my mom all those many months. In the spring of 2009, I was laid off after 15 years. Now, I wasn't the only one holding a pink slip—the dip in the economy was taking its toll on the whole industry—but I suspected all those hours away at the hospital pushed my name onto the list of people to be let go. I didn't have any regrets, mind you, but I was awfully scared. The last thing I needed after so many difficult months was the loss of a steady paycheck.

Then my sister Peggy had this suggestion, "Think of this as an opportunity. Now you can do book launches full time and set your own hours!" Peggy has a great way of seeing the best in situations, and she got me so pumped up that I trademarked my new company's name, Hasmark Services, the same day. Everything was going to be okay—that's the attitude I chose to take.

"There are two ways to live your life. One is as though nothing is a miracle. The other is as though everything is a miracle."
—Albert Einstein.

But then, there was Snickers. He was Gerry's dog, and had joined our mixed family. I loved having Snickers around. The house was too quiet with mom gone. But within a couple weeks, our furry little cockapoo came back from the groomer's really mopey and tired. We called the groomer to ask whether Snickers had accidentally been medicated. The groomer insisted that she hadn't done anything that might have caused Snickers' change in behavior. What could have happened?

Cancer.

Our vet broke the news to us a few days later. And a month to the day after I lost my job, we lost Snickers too. Hadn't I had enough crying and sadness for one year?

Determined to move forward with positivity, I put my energies into building up Hasmark Services and traveling with Gerry. We loved a good adventure together! Often, we got together with our families for dinner and outings.

On February 16th, 2010, Gerry and I received a call from his sister Marlene telling us that their sister Evelyn had just survived a heart attack and was in the hospital. Wow. We were totally not expecting that blow. Gerry and I hurried to join the rest of the family at the hospital and hoped for the best news. Evelyn had just turned 60, so we figured with the quick medical attention, she'd recover soon and simply have to make some lifestyle changes and take some medications. Then everything would be back to normal, right?

But in the course of doing tests, the doctors discovered she had Stage IV lung cancer.

She was gone a week later.

I was in a daze as the whole family comforted each other and tried to take in what had just happened. Gerry was their rock, assuring everyone that we would be okay. His unwavering strength reminded me of why I loved him so much. After so many years on my own, it felt so good to know that I was married to a strong man who loved his family and mine and who could always be counted on in a crisis.

"Our strongest connections with others are created through the depths of our sorrows, not by the peaks of our happiness."
—Sheila Tilotta

As the weeks passed, Marlene mentioned more than once that she felt fatigued. At first, of course, we all assumed it was due to having lost her sister so unexpectedly and being in a state of grief. But she said, "I feel it's something more than that. Something's not quite right with me. I'm thinking I should see the doctor." Marlene's always been a strong person with lots of energy, so this was unusual. We knew how important it was that she get some tests. Plus, she had a heart condition, so we figured she might need some medication adjustments, or maybe even bypass surgery. Gerry and I didn't let ourselves be pessimistic, but after losing Evelyn and my Mom to cancer, I had to make an effort not to "go there" and start thinking, "what if--?" It wasn't going to do anyone any good to think negatively.

Gerry and I were happy to help her out driving her to the doctors again and again for test after test. In between we took short trips to local areas to enjoy time together. We continued our weekly shopping trips where we laughed and bought silly things.

All the tests were inconclusive until August, when she learned she had a kidney stone. Well, that was a relief! Something simple and treatable! I felt bad that Marlene was in a lot of pain but glad that she would soon be on the mend.

Then, Marlene began to complain of arm pain, and saying, "Something's still not right." I don't know why some people have a strong intuition about themselves and their health, but Marlene clearly was picking up on something the doctors were missing.

Her intuition was right.

Marlene became so weak she could barely function. We arranged for all the recommended tests to be done on the same day. At last, we were lead into the oncologist's office and the news was delivered to all of us.

She had Stage IV lung cancer.

The doctors were able to remove some fluid around her heart, which was crushing it. With that, her pain lifted and her energy was boosted, but the cancer had spread.

We prepared ourselves.

"Be thankful for the difficult times. During those times you grow."
—Author unknown

Winter moved in. It was difficult to believe that cancer had so profoundly affected our family. We didn't know how many days Marlene had left, but Gerry was determined to see her as often as we could and to lend assistance by driving her, helping her out at home, and giving her emotional support. I know his unwavering strength was helping build her courage as she fought her battle.

The months passed and Marlene hung on. We were pleasantly surprised when she returned to work at the beginning of 2011. We wanted to believe this was a good sign that she would beat the disease. In fact, Gerry and I packed up and went on a trip to Key West, Florida. Driving down the Gulf

Coast was great fun as we stopped to see the gators on the side of the road. Gerry was like a little kid, getting out of the car at every sighting.

Two days after returning home in February we were met with a beautiful snowfall. While Gerry started up our snow blower to clear our walkway and sidewalk in the front, I grabbed a shovel and slowly began to dig out a path for Bailey. Gerry appeared at the door and asked me to come into the house. I went in and found Gerry sitting on the couch. He didn't look right.

"What's up?" I asked.

"I don't know. I feel a heaviness in my chest. I thought I'd better sit for a while and see if it goes away."

"Maybe we should call 911?"

"No, I'm sure it'll pass. Don't worry."

But it didn't pass and after thirty minutes, I convinced him to let me dial 911.

Although his symptoms were subtle—none of that dramatic gasping and grabbing the chest that you see on television—it turns out Gerry had suffered a heart attack. The doctors reassured us that because we had called the ambulance soon after he started feeling unwell and gotten him to the hospital quickly, the damage to his heart was minimal. They inserted a stent and he was feeling better within hours.

I will never forget the call I had to make to his sister, Marlene. Here she was dealing with having lost their sister the year before, her terminal diagnosis and now her beloved brother in the hospital having suffered a heart attack. "I'm coming to see him" she said immediately knowing she could barely walk herself. My heart broke as I knew she relied on him so very much for her own care, for her own children, and to be her executor.

Thank goodness his diagnosis was positive!

He was told to rest for a couple of weeks and return for some more tests to see how his recovery was going.

I said a prayer of gratitude. After so many losses, losing my husband would be devastating. I was deeply thankful that he was going to be okay and we could continue our life together. We were in grief about Marlene's grim prognosis, of course, but she had a very good attitude, and we would continue to be there for her.

When you have a heart attack, the doctors insist on running many tests to be sure that all your systems are okay. So off to the doctor's Gerry went, while I waited in the car. When he returned, I asked,

"Any news? Do we have to pick up a prescription?"

"There's a spot on my lung," he said.

I looked at him in horror.

"It's just a spot, they say—so tiny we shouldn't worry. Even if it is cancer, we need to focus on my heart getting stronger. Then they can do a biopsy. It could be pneumonia or something else. Let's just think positive."

As soon as we got the actual results, I read them to get more answers. "Mild associated volume loss…thin halo of ground glass opacity…visualized intra-abdominal viscera are normal." Oh boy. I hoped we could get an explanation in clear English, but when we talked to the doctors, the bottom line was, "We just can't tell yet whether it's malignant." That I understood and could hold on to as we went through the merry-go-round of tests and labs and doctors' offices and clinics.

Enjoy Your Life While You Can

Gerry trusted his doctors, and they didn't seem worried, so I tried not to be anxious about the "spot." Testing began and with each appointment, it became harder to rule out cancer. In fact, we kept our hopes so high that Gerry went to one appointment without me, sure he'd hear the usual: "It's inconclusive so we'll have to run another test." Eventually, we were so frustrated with the delays in getting tests that we set up a CT scan at a different hospital, but it wasn't until he was strong enough to withstand a bronchoscopy (a very invasive test) that we finally learned the nature of the spot.

Malignant.

I was speechless. I really had tried to have faith. I couldn't believe that this time, we got a solid answer—and it was the worst one possible. Gerry and I hugged each other and cried.

After that, the doctors told us lung surgery would be scheduled for May 31. They were hoping that his heart would be strong enough by then to handle the powerful anesthesia and the stress to his system. So, on May 30, we were preparing Gerry to go into the hospital the next day. All the tests had been run and pre-op appointments had been completed, and we were expecting to spend the summer focused on his healing.

Then the phone rang. It was the surgeon calling to cancel the operation. "I don't understand," I said.

"The cancer grew more quickly than we expected. And some of it is outside of the lung. Stage III lung cancer. We're suggesting aggressive chemotherapy and radiation," he told us grimly. "We'd like to reschedule surgery for August 15. Hopefully, by then the spot will be small enough that we can take it out, and we'll have cleared any of the cancer that has metastasized."

The news left us numb. I'd heard the words clearly enough, but my brain couldn't make sense of them—or maybe it was my heart that refused to accept what they meant.

The "tiny" spot had grown like a weed while we'd plodded away, dutifully following the doctor's orders to get Gerry plenty of rest. It had won the race of time, and now we were going to have to go into battle for Gerry's life.

Three weeks later, an aggressive regimen of chemotherapy and radiation began. The medication piled up on the counter, side effects were discussed in detail, and the local cancer clinic did their best to help us understand what we were going to experience.

It was going to be a battle.

Within you is the Strength to Meet Life's Challenges

By now, Marlene was so sick that she couldn't drive. Gerry and I were running back and forth between her bedside, our house, and the clinic where Gerry was getting the chemotherapy. Marlene's daughter, Kelly, drove her mother to appointments when she could, but Marlene was getting weaker and weaker.

I thought about our plans to travel with Marlene. Would she make it, and come with us? Right after we had watched the doctors remove Evelyn's breathing tube and seen her pass peacefully, Marlene, Gerry, and I gathered in the hospital waiting room that had become far too familiar to us and discussed taking a trip together to Africa. Maybe it sounds strange, but at that moment, we all had a powerful need to imagine a future for ourselves filled with life, adventure, and happy times together. We knew Evelyn would have wanted us to embrace life—even give it a bear hug for her.

That memory came back to me as we prayed by Marlene's side. I held on to hope, but unfortunately, we lost her on July 13. With unwavering strength, Gerry held her hand as she passed away, deeply saddened by losing another dear family member. That same day, he drove to the clinic for his own treatment.

Marlene's funeral was an echo of Evelyn's, with many of the same people gathering in quiet shock to say good-bye to Marlene. Gerry was very weak, but he made it through the service and reception. I'm sure having his second sister pass away from cancer in little more than a year was a major blow to him. His heart had been physically weakened. Now, it was aching with emotional pain.

Even so, Gerry and I trudged along going from appointment to appointment, test after test, to prepare him for surgery. We each had a job: I worried and he reassured me! In all seriousness, I wished I were as confident and strong as he was, but I have a harder time letting go of anxiety than Gerry ever did. Every day, we hoped the phone would not ring with a call telling us that surgery had been cancelled again.

When the doctor's office did contact us a week before surgery, it was to let us know that Gerry's pre-surgery tests revealed a blood clot in his lung. We were told it would have to be dissolved with blood thinners so we needed to get to a hospital immediately for treatment. OMG not again! They can't cancel surgery again. Time is not our friend. If they cancel he will surely lose his battle.

At 4:00 a.m. we left the hospital feeling hopeful again. They believed the clot would dissolve and he could continue with the surgery as planned. The doctors continued to seem very optimistic. Wanting to share their mood, I told myself everything would be okay.

That same day, Gerry had an appointment with his doctor and told him he was having some back pain, which his GP noted without much comment. Gerry needed some more preoperative tests so we headed to the hospital cafeteria, got a coffee, and began to pass the time. Unfortunately, Gerry's back pain suddenly got worse. In fact, it became so agonizing within minutes that he collapsed. I guess if you're going to collapse in pain, the place to do it is the hospital cafeteria, because we had more than a dozen doctors and nurses surrounding us within seconds. I tried not to worry as they wheeled him into the ER to get him some painkillers and start the round of tests. We were stunned when they told us he not only had one blood clot, but two (one in each lung). "The surgery was going to be cancelled" said the ER doctor. "The only way to save him was to give him an intense dose of blood thinners. With that major surgery would have to be postponed."

Tests, tests, and more tests. After five long days, my nerves were so shot that I felt as wobbly as a bowl of Jell-O. If they give him too much blood thinner, he would not be ready for surgery, and the cancer would progress. If they did not give him enough, the blood clot would kill him. Here we were again waiting for a diagnosis that would change our lives. Finally, after a filter was surgically inserted in his leg, they released him. And yes, surgery was still on. I took a moment and said a simple prayer thanking God for two days' respite as we went home to wait for Monday and Gerry's long-delayed surgery.

Gerry came through with no complications, but his recovery was slow. I wrote it off to all the stress he'd been under and the pressure on his damaged heart. Weeks passed, with more tests, and it seemed he was clear of cancer. Gerry rallied in October, which made me more hopeful. The doctors said they wanted to do more chemotherapy—"just as a precaution." I hung on to those words.

We kept up the chemotherapy and radiation, and Gerry rallied. We were determined that he was going to be the one family member who battled and won. We kept telling family and friends, "Thank goodness he had a heart attack, as it probably saved his life."

"A hero is an ordinary individual who finds the strength to persevere and endure in spite of overwhelming obstacles."
—Christopher Reeve

November arrived and Gerry started to notice that his legs were getting weaker. We arrived home one evening from being out of town and suddenly, he was in tremendous pain. By the next morning, he was unable to walk. Back to the ER we went . . . more tests with no results. I had to wonder, "How could he be in this much pain, unable to walk, if it is nothing to worry about?" So we went to see his GP, who suggested the symptoms were side effects of chemotherapy. And that's when we received another phone call.

"You need to get to the ER. They saw something on the x-ray," the woman from the hospital told me.

At the ER, we learned that the cancer had shown up in his bones, which explained why it had become so hard for him to walk. Aggressive chemotherapy and radiation followed. This time, I pushed for him to get treatment as soon as possible. I was not going to be timid when my husband's life was at stake!

The next few weeks were a blur as I tried to hold on to hope. Just before Christmas, the doctors made it clear to the two of us that the cancer was simply too aggressive. The likelihood of Gerry beating it had faded, and we needed to prepare ourselves to lose him to lung cancer. Gerry said nothing as the doctor left the room. We held each other. What was there to say at this point, except, "I love you?"

I was committing to staying positive, but something had been weighing on me for quite a while. I finally found the courage to bring up a difficult subject.

"Gerry," I said, "if this doesn't work . . . I mean, if the worst happens . . . maybe we should talk—"

Gerry cut me off abruptly. "I don't want to talk. You know what I want."

I did. When Evelyn died and Marlene got sick, we inevitably started to ponder what we would do if we were ever in the terrible situation of facing an early death. I wanted to connect with him over the difficult truth that he might not make it, but then I realized that at this point, he couldn't handle the conversation. After all, he had sat at the bedside of one person after another as they fought cancer. He saw the devastating effect cancer has on the body. I honestly have no idea how he didn't lose his mind.

One day while on the phone with Peggy, all of us discussed the option of going to Florida for the month of January. Gerry loved the idea. Peggy and her husband, Denis, would be there in the event anything went wrong and promised to help shoulder some of the care if Gerry felt very weak. We began to pack seconds after he received a chemo treatment and then headed down to Spring Hill. We had a great time going to Disney World and Busch Gardens, golfing, and reconnecting with Gerry's one remaining sibling, Yvonne, who lived nearby. Spending those weeks in Florida was a bright light in the middle of a storm. We were also looking forward to trips to Whistler, British Columbia and New Orleans after our return home. There was so much to see and do, and so much living to get in.

Gerry was strong enough to play a few rounds of golf, and Peggy and Denis were taking time out to shop for a vacation home. I got to thinking about Gerry and my plans for retiring here.

"Maybe we should start looking for a house now," I said to him one day. "The prices are low and the interest rates are fantastic."

Gerry smiled sadly at me. "It's up to you, Judy. Chances are I'll only be here for a short time, so you'd probably be in it alone…"

I choked up. I'd wanted so badly to plan our future, and enjoy believing that we had one together despite the odds against him. But I guess in that moment, Gerry felt the need to be honest about his chances. I just wanted to believe that everything would be okay.

I didn't bring up the house again.

*"I look at life as a gift of God. Now that he wants it back
I have no right to complain"*

—Joyce Cary

Shortly after we returned, the cancer spread to Gerry's brain. We cancelled our trip to Mardi Gras in New Orleans and the vacation in Whistler, BC. It became clear it was time to bring Gerry's children home.

I told him that his daughter, Katie, was coming from Calgary, and he insisted that wasn't possible because she had to work. "No, Gerry, she's coming. She wants to be with you." His face just lit up when he saw her. And when his son, Nick, arrived, you could just feel the joy radiating from him. And for the first time in weeks he came to the dinner table, even though he had completely lost his appetite. We'd tried to get him to eat nutritional shakes, McDonald hamburgers—his favorite—and everything we could think of that might make him eat to keep up his stamina. But it seems having both his kids with him was what was giving him the most strength.

I knew he didn't want to die in a hospital. We brought a bed into the living room and we began taking care of him night and day. In April, he seemed to be near the end.

And then, Gerry slipped into a coma. Nick, Katie, and I waited silently. Our family and friends checked in by e-mail and phone and told us that they were praying for us. We waited silently as a day passed, then two, then three. He opened his eyes and looked at Nick and Katie, but couldn't speak. We told him we loved him, and saw a tear gently glide down his cheek. He closed his eyes again. We waited quietly. Katie, Nick, and I sat by his side, Kate and I each holding one of Gerry's hands. Bailey lay on the bed curled up next to him. And then, my soul mate slipped away at six in the morning on April 10th, 2012.

It still doesn't quite feel real to me. Even after our celebration service for Gerry, after our "official" good-bye, I can't believe he's not with me.

And I can't believe the power cancer has had to take away so many of the people I loved, and in such a short time.

"Perhaps they are not stars, but rather openings in heaven where the love of our lost ones pours through and shines down upon us to let us know they are happy."
—Eskimo Proverb

Two and a half months later, my daughter Amy's best friend, Carrie, a young mother with two small children, lost her own two-year battle to skin cancer. As soon as I got the news, my heart broke for Amy and for Carrie's family. I knew how this fight can wear you down in so many different ways. Like Amy, I did what I could to lend support. Several of Carrie's friends and relatives had put together a fundraiser to pay for an experimental treatment in Mexico when the doctors said they had exhausted all their own tools for bringing her back to health. The treatment didn't work, but the experience made me feel much less helpless—and I was tired of feeling helpless in the face of cancer.

I remember when Gerry was sick, I instant messaged my sister, Peggy, one day to say, "I feel the need to do something for other families." I was becoming an expert on how to help a loved one with cancer—something I never wanted to be. But if I had to learn what I was learning, maybe someday I could share what I knew with others and keep them from feeling overwhelmed.

During Gerry's final days, I started thinking about writing this book. I designed a cover in Gerry's favorite color, green, and showed it to him, Katie, and Nick the evening before he passed away.

Rhonda (Evelyn's daughter) and Katie said they'd like to do something in his honor, too—and to honor Marlene and Evelyn. We came up with the idea of an organization to raise funds and offer support and information to families of cancer patients. We decided to name it G.E.M. after the O'Beirn siblings: Gerry, Evelyn, and Marlene. We have just gotten started with all our plans, and many of our relatives and friends are on board to help us organize fundraisers and spread the word that it is possible to get through this experience with unwavering strength.

Soon, I will have to face what would have been Gerry and my fifth anniversary. It's hard not to cry when I think about how we meant to spend it on a boat somewhere—maybe the Caribbean, or Alaska. I feel like getting a boat and sinking it! I met the perfect husband and then cancer ripped him away from me. Sometimes, I just get really angry about it. That's when I take a deep breath and start working on my G.E.M. projects. I figure that's better than going completely crazy with grief, or sitting down and saying, "Woe is me." A pity party doesn't make me feel any better. Besides, I have people counting on me—including the readers of this book, and the families I have yet to meet who will benefit from what G.E.M. will do for them.

I think we all need to find something that will keep us feeling strong on those days when it's really hard not to give in to anger and sadness. It was especially difficult in those first weeks after the memorial service, when there was nothing left to do: no arrangements to make, no calls to relatives to ensure that they were up on the latest news. I'd been going like the Energizer Bunny for so long that I hadn't had time to take in all the losses I'd experienced. That's when it hit me the hardest.

Sometimes, people would apologize if they brought up Gerry's name, thinking I didn't want to hear it, but I'd tell them it was far worse not to hear it. I don't ever want to forget how wonderful he was and how much joy he brought into my life. So, even though it's painful, I want to talk about him. People will just have to accept that it's hard for me to do without crying, but friends and family understand. That's the great thing about the people you love. They let you be yourself even when you're a weepy mess.

So I've kept going. And each day gets a tiny bit easier.

I am determined each morning when I wake up to make sure that I get up, get out, and do what I can. And on the worst days, I choose to be inspired by Gerry and all the other cancer patients who taught me you just have to keep fighting, keep going, and keep hoping. You have to remember that there are people who want to help—even strangers. No one has to go through this alone. And take comfort in knowing that by sharing my story with you, I might just be able to make you feel that you can get through this, too.

I know you can.

Epilogue

It has been two years since Gerry passed away and since then this book has become an important focus in my life. I have to tell you that it has been a roller coaster ride. Just when you think that the crying and sobbing is over it starts all over again.

Shortly after Gerry's service someone told me that I had not mourned all my losses. I thought, "What are you talking about, I certainly miss them and have done my share of crying," but boy were they right. I have never felt anything so deep or so strong.

I wrote this book for you! And selfishly for me. I need to talk about my journey. I need others to know that there is light at the end of the darkest and longest of tunnels. And to find purpose to why I was chosen to have this journey. And most importantly, almost more important than anything else, is "What can I do for others that will make it a tiny wee bit easier to get through a similar life event. And how can I honor those who are gone."

It is your choice how you deal with the life you have been given. You can wallow in it or you can choose to honor your loved one's memory and do something for someone else unselfishly. I read a book by Dr Terry A Gordon called No Storm Lasts Forever in which Terry went through a life changing event and his message was to not dwell on the worst of the situation, but be thankful for what you have.

The most important message I have for you is that "You are not alone."

About the Author

Judy O'Beirn has spent the last seven years helping hundreds of authors become bestsellers in her role as president of Hasmark Services. More recently she has become an author and Creator of a book of short stories titled 'Unwavering Strength.' She decided to write the book when her husband, Gerry, became ill with cancer and ultimately passed away from the disease in 2012, to help her channel her grief. In the two previous years before she lost him, she lost her mother, two sister-in-laws, her dog, and her daughters' best friend all to the disease, and a brother years before that. Her goal for this book is to help others deal with loss in their lives. She has organized two golf tournaments to raise money for families affected by cancer and is currently planning the next one. Visit *Unwavering Strength* to become an Ambassador of *Unwavering Strength*.

H.O.P.E.

Kellie Bishop

"Being deeply loved by someone gives you strength, while loving someone deeply gives you courage."
—Lao Tzu

It was a random Tuesday, in the wee hours of a July morning, when I was awakened by the telephone call from my sister. "Kel, where's Brittany?" I replied that she was spending the night with a girlfriend. "Are you sure?" My heart began to race and I asked "Why, Kim?" She told me that a friend had just phoned. There was an accident in front of her friend's house, on a country road several miles from our home. The friend's daughter thought she heard the paramedics say Brittany's name.

Brittany is my daughter. At that time she was about two weeks shy of her 17th birthday and a month away from beginning her senior year of high school.

I jumped from my bed and ran down the stairs. I tried to reach Brittany on her cell phone. I dialed her number over and over, but only got her voice-mail recording. "Brittany, please answer the phone, honey. I won't be mad. I promise! I just need to hear your voice." Those were the words running through my mind. It was summertime. Britt told me that she and a few other girls were having a sleepover. They were going to stay in and watch movies. She wasn't supposed to be in a car!

My husband, Beau came to the kitchen and asked me what in the world was going on. I told him what Kim had said. I wanted to drive to where the car accident was reported to be. Beau wouldn't let me go. I called the police and a friend who was the Chief of the volunteer fire department. No one would answer my questions. I'm generally a calm person, but my stomach

20

was churning and my heart was pounding furiously. I felt like a caged animal. I was boxed in, bouncing off the walls waiting for an answer and looking for an escape from the panic that was setting in.

Hours later, before the dawn, two police officers parked in front of our home. I ran out to meet them and ask where Brittany was, how Brittany was. They asked if anyone else was home and if they could come inside. Our son, Ryan, was 13 years old. He and his cousin, Will, were at Walt Disney World with my mother. My husband and I were home alone.

I expected them to tell me Brittany had been in an automobile accident and was injured but that she'd be fine. They sat down at the kitchen table with Beau and me, where they presented a brown paper bag. The bag was the size I used to pack my children's school lunch. Inside the bag was a shoe, one familiar platform sandal. There was an ankle bracelet broken into two pieces and there was a silver wrist cuff covered with dirt.

I'm looking at that bag now. We've kept it for some reason. Those were Brittany's things. When we acknowledged that the contents belonged to our daughter, one of the policemen began to tell us that Brittany was in a fatal crash. I don't recall the exact words. I can't tell you what either officer looked like. They said there were three girls in the car. Brittany was in the back seat.

Brittany was never in the back seat. She always called "shotgun." The driver and other passenger were in the hospital. My only recollection of the rest of their stay was the uncontrollable shaking that overcame my body and the physical pain of feeling my heart break, silently cracking into pieces within the walls of my chest. I wanted to die. I wanted to be with Brittany. I wanted to see my daughter. I didn't believe them. There had to be a mistake, but no one would take me to her!

I went to Brittany's room, sat on the floor and cried desperate, uncontrollable, wrenching tears; the pain-filled tears of knowing life would never be the same; the tears of imagining that I would never hold my daughter again or hear her laughter. I knew I could never laugh again.

Brittany's room was where my sister found me. She gently told me that I had to call my mom and that I had to tell Ryan. I didn't want to call them. I wanted to let them finish their vacation and tell them when they got home. Kim gently convinced me that I couldn't do that. I finally picked up the phone and made a telephone call that still haunts me when I think about it. I said it was a "random" Tuesday. It wasn't. It was my mother's birthday. I had to call my mother on her birthday to tell her that her granddaughter was dead and to tell my son his sister was gone. I wanted to be with Ryan and hold him and whisper in his ear that everything would be all right; that we would be all right. I remember looking up from the floor and asking my sister, "What do you do with the rest of your life when you're 43 and the best of it is already over?"

Word spreads quickly among teenagers. Within hours Brittany's friends had organized a candlelight ceremony in the cul-de-sac in front of our home. That very first evening without Britt, our family gathered in our front yard in amazement as a group of more than 300 people came together to share their compassion. There were friends, neighbors, and perfect strangers playing music, embracing Ryan, telling stories, and sharing their love in the only way they knew how. They wanted to comfort us. When everyone left, I found a beautiful, ornate, silver cross pendant on a long chain. When I placed it around my neck, the chain reached down long enough for the cross to sit on my chest . . . on my heart, and I said aloud, "I wish I had the kind of faith that could carry me now." I was wishing for the deep connection with God that I imagined the sweet soul who left that cross must have had.

In the days that followed we received cards that said the sender was holding us in their prayers. My prayer was to make the nightmare end, to make my family whole again.

I read, "Grief is a physical, social, emotional, psychological, and spiritual reaction to loss. It is natural, normal, and necessary." You don't get over it. You get through it. So the journey began.

Each morning I woke thinking about our son, Ryan. I had to get up and put one foot in front of the other to make sure Ryan was okay." . . . loving someone deeply gives you courage." Beau and I didn't talk about how we were going to survive. We didn't talk about the agonizing pain and despair. It would have broken one or both of us. " . . . being deeply loved by someone gives you strength".

At Brittany's memorial, my husband spoke. He asked all of the teens to take out their cell phones and add our telephone number. He promised them a safe ride home, no questions asked, if they'd just call him. From that, was born the foundation he and other family members created. The foundation, B.R.I.T.T. (Beats Risking It, Take a Taxi) paid taxi rides home for local teenagers. Beau spoke to driver's education students at the local high schools for several years.

After getting Ryan off to school in the morning, I spent hours reading, walking, seeking solace, and searching for directions to heal my heart. Before a flight takes off from the ground, a flight attendant gives safety instructions. They say if there is a loss of cabin pressure oxygen masks will drop from the overhead compartment. The most important part of the message is that in order to help someone else you must first put on your own oxygen mask. Taking time each morning to seek greater knowledge and understanding was what helped me breathe.

One evening, two years after the accident, I was having dinner with some women on my husband's side of the family. This was an unusual gathering. We didn't often see each other. My husband's cousin, whom I had only met a couple of times, was directly across from me. While everyone around us was engaged in conversation, she looked at me and sweetly said, "Your angel is always with you, isn't she?" I told her I thought she was. She went on, "I have a message for you. She loves what you've done with her room." A big smile came across her face and a single tear ran down mine. Nothing had changed in Brittany's room . . . until that week. I had moved her bed and replaced her comforter with something bright and new. No one, including Beau and Ryan, knew that except me! I recalled that family members told me this cousin was an intuitive. I hadn't ever given it a thought. This was the beginning of my healing. I received a message from heaven! They say a broken heart is an open heart. An open heart and open mind have allowed me to receive even more messages, which had opened a whole new world to me.

A young friend recommended a book called Conversations with God by Neale Donald Walsch. That book helped me to understand that God wasn't mad or punishing me. Forgiveness was a critical milestone.

Compassion. Love. Faith. Prayer. Forgiveness. Peace. This was the tonic that healed my heart and brought me the courage to carry on. Looking back over the past eleven years it seems so much clearer.

- Compassion, from loved ones or strangers, is love.

- Love is healing.

- Faith erases fear.

- Prayer is the loving energy that people send from their heart to buoy us.

- Forgiveness is understanding.

- Knowing that life continues after we leave this ground is peace.

Together they give me unwavering strength.

"Imagine we are astronauts who have crashed on the moon. We look across the vastness of space and see the beautiful blue Earth. But we can't get back because our ship is damaged. All we can do is look at that brilliant blue beautiful orb in the black sky and dream of being home.

But suppose we managed to fix our ship, and landed back home. How would we feel when we first set foot upon the Earth? What would we observe and savor? How intensely would we experience the sights and smells, the flavors, the feeling of a gentle rain?

That's how we should walk on the Earth with each step."

A WALKING EXERCISE FROM THICH NHAT HANH

This is what I owe my daughter, to enjoy each step, to live with purpose and love and to share HOPE from my grateful heart. Brittany's middle name is Hope, which is now an acronym: *Holding Only Positive Energy*.

Hope brought me faith and faith gave me H.O.P.E.

Brittany gave me a little piece of paper when she was nine years old. My father was dying and she knew how sad I was. The little note had a smiley face and the words, "Smile for me." I carry this note with me and I am smiling, Sweetheart!

I have a daughter who was involved in an automobile accident. I was told she didn't survive. This is not the truth. My sweet angel Brittany is alive. She lives in my heart.

About the Author

Kellie Bishop lives in Charlottesville, Virginia with her husband and their black lab, Riley.

She is a full time travel consultant in her own agency. Kellie is an avid traveler herself and believes travel expands her awareness and compassion. When her son moved to Mississippi for law school, Kellie felt another profound life changing experience, an empty nest. This propelled Kellie to explore, within, more deeply to find her purpose. She knows that happiness is an inside job and life is a gift. She shares messages to provoke thought and inspire HOPE. Please visit www.InKelliesWorld.com.

Believe

Brian Bogardus

"Every storm runs out of rain."
—Gary Allan

September 13

It's 3 a.m., I am finally home. You are already asleep and the TV is on. I curl up next to you in bed. You smile and let out a faint "mmmm . . ."

I didn't know that would be the last response I'd ever hear from you.

October 10

Raquel, I hope that someday you'll be able to read this. I'm spending the night across the hall, in an empty patient room in the neuro care unit. Our lives were forever changed 27 days ago.

You looked run-down the morning after I got home from that business trip. I popped my head in while you were showering to see if you were OK. Sitting on the shower floor, you were grabbing your head, crying out that it was the worst pain you'd ever felt. Four seconds later, you lost consciousness.

Massive aneurysm.

Tufts Medical Center is now our home. When I first arrived at Tufts, I was told that your bleed was "spectacular" and that you went into cardiac arrest. "Not going to make it . . .", "if she somehow does . . .", "don't see her living beyond a few days . . .", "the odds are against her . . .", "she'll never be the same person. . . ."

I don't know how to make sense of our new reality.

Raq, this has been the most brutal thing that I've ever been through. It is beyond physical pain . . . it tears at my soul. My heart breaks for our boys. Our 18- and 24-year-old sons shouldn't have to see their mom go through this.

You open your eyes, but there's no response from you, baby. Can you hear us?

I'm so mad that this has happened to you. You're such a beautiful person with a heart of gold.

October 22

Raq, you're still in a minimally conscious state. Our object is to get you off the ventilator. Stay strong baby. It kills me to have to leave you each night.

I just want you back home. We've got a long way to go. They say it will take three to six months to know if you'll be OK. It's going to be a long and grueling road for everybody, but we're up for the challenge.

Raquel, the outpouring of love, support, and prayer has been unbelievable. Hundreds of people are pulling for you, many who don't even know us.

It's a lonely place at home without you, especially at night. You're not there for me to wrap around. You have to come home. You've had plenty of opportunity to die, and you haven't. I'm not giving up hope.

So, Raq, explain this. This afternoon I whispered in your ear, "Honey, I know you can hear me. I know you can't comunicate, but that's OK." Just then, my phone rang. I pulled it out of my pocket, entered my passcode, and saw that it was YOUR phone calling! How could that happen?

When I got home I googled the meaning of 256 (2:56 was the time my phone rang.) I was shocked . . . the 256th day of the year is Sept. 13th, the day you left us. I think it's a sign that you'll be home soon. I love you with all my heart and soul. The boys need you back, I need you back.

October 26

The odds are stacked against you. Please come back to us. I have heard your voice every day for 26 years, I'm not used to this silence. This is the deepest, darkest place I've ever been.

Your roommate beat cancer six years ago and now it has come back with a vengeance. She writes on her white board how lonely and scared she is.

I pray that you're not scared, not in pain. I pray for our boys, that they'll persevere.

Everyone says "stay strong" but after hearing it so many times, I just want to say, "You f***ing try to stay strong through this!" It's brutal. We have faith in God, but I don't understand the why.

It is teaching me mental toughness like nothing else. It's teaching me to focus on what's important . . . friends and family. It's teaching me to not worry about the small stuff. It's teaching me that the love you have in your life is what's important. Oh God, I think I've taken so much for granted. I'm so sorry.

All the money in the world can't bring you back and I hate that.

Raq, we don't ever say "goodbye." We always say "later." "Later" implies a next time, without regard to time. Good night, sweetheart. Later, baby.

December 9

Raq, another aneurysm and you skirted with death again. We are at Spaulding Rehab now, mourning the person that you were, because you'll never, ever, be the same.

Today is Austin's 19th birthday. The boys miss talking with you. The depth of my missing you is crushing me. I see how much the boys hurt. I am trying to be spiritual and positive, but this roller coaster of emotion makes it so hard.

I feel like I'm living a bad dream. Please God, let me wake up. This is so surreal.

They say that we still have a chance at getting you home. You'll be different, but will you'll still be you? I pray that there's a glimmer of you in there . . . that spark of who you were.

I know that tragic events happen daily. You always wonder why. I want to believe that there's a purpose to them. Every patient's room, every life, has a story to be told.

December 26

They say you're not conscious of anything. So much of you is lost. Reality is sinking in and it sucks.

January 10

Raq, we had a very difficult family meeting today. There is damage to every part of your brain, which means no chance of a functional recovery.

I'm so lost right now. God, give me strength to accept this brutal reality.

I know you wouldn't want to live in this vegetative state. Your physical body is here but you are not. You have to be turned and changed every two hours. To keep you in this state between life and death, in between the two worlds isn't fair. Maybe one of the greatest gifts I can give you is to let you go. I'm not sure I know how to.

I love you Raq. I'll never find another you, nor do I want to. I'm going to miss growing old with you. I'll miss the beach, the back deck . . . so many things. The depth of sorrow and loss is beyond comprehension.

Life isn't fair but I'm beginning to sense that there must be reasons why things happen. If I had come back one day later from that business trip, you would've died and one of the boys would've found you. I cannot fathom that.

I believe that maybe there's a purpose to the timing of all this. If this happened earlier in our lives it would've been much more difficult for the boys. And if it happened later in life, it would've been so much more difficult for me. Maybe it's the right time for this to happen. God does that even make sense?

February 11

No improvement, not good.

I've prayed and pleaded for a miracle to get you home. I prayed to God to bring you back for just one minute so you could tell me to let you go.

Maybe this long goodbye is giving everyone a chance to come together. Maybe it's to help us all appreciate what we have. Maybe it's to offer everyone a chance to say their goodbyes in their own way and to help us adjust to life without you.

I don't know where this road is leading us, but we believe life continues after death, so I know that you'll be there for us in spirit and that gives me comfort.

March 8

You're still not making any progress and as much as I don't like it, I've begun to accept it. It's selfish to leave you in this state, locked in your body, in this bed, unable to get out and enjoy life. I won't leave you like this, baby. We're starting to talk about the steps to help you to transition.

The boys and I have gone through hell. I'm so sad that this is the end of our physical journey. We've had a great 26 years together. We stood the test of time. This next month will be excruciatingly painful. I never imagined our journey would bring us to this.

I believe that God has a purpose for everything and that gives me unwavering strength. I want to do some wonderful things in your memory. I pray to God every day for strength so that we can touch many people through our experience.

April 2

Raq, we fought the good fight. You waited for me and the boys to arrive. Cody kept his hand on your heart, and Austin was on the other side holding you. I was draped across your legs. We felt your last physical moments . . . watched your last breaths. Cody felt your last heartbeat. Soul ripping pain juxtaposed with tears of joy. You are free. I wonder if you were aware of the journey we were all on.

Brian . . . I heard every word from you, the boys, and from everyone who came in, wrote in, or called in. The overwhelming amount of pain you all felt was equal to the overwhelming amount of love that I felt. There's the irony in it, Brian . . . the darkness within the light and the light within the darkness. You wanted to bring me home . . . and you did. Your love brought me to my spiritual home, which is infinitely connected to you. I'm so proud of you, Code and Austin. To all who are reading this . . . home is in your heart . . . always look there. Don't stop believing.

Final thoughts . . .

My wish for each of you is this: Be fully present in every relationship. Appreciate people's little quirks. Slow down and say "I love you and I appreciate you." You never know when it will be your last opportunity to say it to them face to face. One of the greatest gifts I received was when a friend told me that he woke up in the middle of the night simply to tell his wife that he loved her, because our story made him re-evaluate life's priorities.

I hope that as you find your way through darkness, it will lead you into new purpose. I hope you realize that any ending is a new beginning. What you do with your new beginning is up to you. I hope you can find purpose in it . . . that will be your unwavering strength.

Much love. Later.

About the Author

Brian Bogardus is a District Sales Manager for Mazda and a sought-after inspirational speaker. Brian's calling is to help others navigate their way through their own darkness to once again experience a life filled with joy and love. He has set up a non-profit foundation, "Raq's Home," to help families affected by acquired or traumatic brain injury and to promote aneurysm awareness. You can find him on facebook at Team Roxy, or email him at Brianbogardus@hotmail.com

The First Seven Years

Emmanuel Dagher

"And one has to understand that braveness is not the absence of fear but rather the strength to keep on going forward despite the fear."
—Paulo Coelho

When I reflect on what unwavering strength means to me, I am instantly transported back to my childhood. You see, unwavering strength is the sole vehicle that brought me to this present point in time, to a place where I am able to share my story with you.

It has often been stated that the first seven years of a person's life are the most critical because that is when the mind is passing through its most delicate developmental stages. This period of time usually becomes the reference point people refer back to as they navigate from childhood into adulthood. During this time, the foundations are laid that will shape who we become as adults.

Looking back at the first seven years of my own childhood, I feel blessed for the lessons that helped me develop a state of unwavering strength. It brought me the gift of being able to experience my ultimate freedom today.

Like most people, my lessons didn't come without their challenges. To give you a better understanding of what I mean, let me tell you a bit of my story.

The first memory I can recall in this lifetime was sitting with my mother on the cold cement floor of a bedroom that belonged to one of the nuns at the convent where we were staying.

I remember singing with my mother, using only our soft whispering voices, because we didn't want to draw any unwanted attention to ourselves.

We had to remain quiet because on the other side of the wall, outside the convent, were sounds and sights that no human being should ever have to experience. These were the sounds and images of the Lebanese Civil War, which reached its peak during the 1980s.

I am still amazed at how blessed we were for even getting safely in through those convent doors because the nuns never opened the doors to anyone who came from outside the church. They knew my mom was a great schoolteacher and so they made an exception and hired her on to assist the other teachers in the school as needed. Of course there wasn't much school going on during those days and we felt there must have been a higher power watching over us. What was also quite extraordinary was that I was the only "boy" there.

Our bed was a thin blanket that we shared. We had no running hot water and minimal electricity. We had one VHS tape, which was The Sound of Music. I think I must have seen that movie a thousand times. It's kind of funny because Maria was going to become a nun at the convent and the movie was set right before WWII so it was similar to our own circumstances. I think that is when my love for music began. We could identify with the character of Maria as such a free spirit, and feeling it within myself was very comforting. That movie helped us get through a lot of rough days.

The convent room I stayed in had a barred window—sort of like the ones in castles back in the day. I would see the war right outside my little window and I had to grow up very quickly. There was a thickness you could feel in the air that had a relentless nauseating affect that did not let up for years.

I can remember being three years old and living amidst the sounds of bombs, tanks, and firefights on the other side of the convent wall. I made a deal with myself then, promising that if my mom and I had the opportunity to make it out safely, that I would spend the rest of my life trying to impact the world in a positive way.

I got through it all by singing, creating magical escape stories with my mom, and saying many prayers. No one talked about the war because we were all living it. It was not something people discussed because it was hard. It sounds strange to most people who have not been through this, but there is an unspoken acknowledgment.

The interesting thing is, although I could feel my mother's fear and the fear of everyone around me at the time, there was always a sense of inner peace and trust that everything was going to be okay. I believe now that these two components of inner peace and trust are what helped me build my own unwavering strength.

In fact, my mom often tells me that it was as if I was her parent most of the time. I would have her rest her head on my shoulder, affirming to her that everything was going to be OK. I would assure her that a greater presence was watching over us and keeping us safe.

She often tells me that those words, along with my ability to make her laugh during the little performances I would put on for her, are what got her through those challenging times.

After several years of living on bread and water, on the floor of a convent bedroom, we were able to escape the combat zone. We used a brief break in the civil war to take a chance on creating a better life for ourselves. To me, leaving the safe haven of the convent was great but also scary because it had been our refuge for so long.

Through a miraculous series of events that could make a book of their own we were able to escape the war and leave Lebanon for a better life. We never looked back.

As hard as this experience was to go through, I would not change any of it in any way, because I know it made me the person I am today.

I often reflect back on that promise I made myself as a little kid. The promise that if my mom and I made it safely out of the war, for the rest of my life I would work to change the world in a positive way.

I have stayed true to that promise, and have chosen a life of service that supports and uplifts the lives of others through my work and humanitarian efforts.

Whenever a challenge comes up in my daily life, I think back to the first seven years of my life and the unwavering strength my experiences taught me.

This immediately puts everything into perspective and reminds me how resilient and blessed I am. It helps me to trust that every challenge in our lives is an opportunity for expansion, a chance to manifest the inner peace and trust that brings out our own unwavering strength, and helps us align more with our greatest potential.

About the Author

Emmanuel Dagher serves as a Personal Growth Catalyst, Transformation Specialist, Intuitive, and Humanitarian. Through his guidance he has had the sincere honor of co-creating positive shifts in the lives of thousands of people around the world. Being of service to others is one of Emmanuel's highest priorities, and he is dedicated to empowering others to live their greatest life. He is an International Bestselling author of the book, Easy Breezy Miracle. http://www.emmanueldagher.com

Courage to Confidence

Cammie Ritchie

*"Courage is not the absence of fear, but rather the judgement that
something else is more important than fear."*
—Ambrose Redmoon

My favorite word is courage. Without it I wouldn't have had the
unwavering strength to do what I did to save my life.

After college I met up with a classmate John in Alberta. He had
been a good friend and the boyfriend of one of my best friends. I was excited
to get the opportunity to travel around with someone who knew what to see
and do in Alberta.

As we traveled from Calgary to Edmonton, John's truck broke down on
the highway. Lucky for us John had a stepbrother in Edmonton who came
and rescued us. We bunked with David for three days while the truck was
being repaired. It wasn't long after that it was apparent David and I had a
connection. He was so charming, handsome, and a hero. I had never met
someone like David before, and feelings stirred in me that were unfamiliar
yet incredibly exciting.

Once I got home to Ontario, David wrote me every day. These were
true love letters, and soon I had fallen in love with the man behind the pen.
We were meant to be together, and so I prepared to move away from home
for the first time and go to Edmonton. Everything was lining up. I had a
good job waiting for me, and David had assured me he had found me a great
apartment.

I arrived in Edmonton late at night after driving for days. David was
kind enough to meet me on the outskirts in a car he had borrowed so I could

follow him to my new apartment. The one bedroom apartment was amazing. I couldn't believe it was mine and that David insisted I not worry about the rent. That's when he told me we would be living there together. My mind started racing, and I came to the conclusion that I must have given him the wrong idea to make him think we would be moving in together. I was sure in our conversations he said he would help me find me my own apartment. I was tired and my emotions of seeing him, being away from home for the first time, and the freedom from my parents had my heading spinning. A good sleep would bring clarity in the morning.

As our day-to-day routine developed I began to follow David's lead since this was how I was raised. I ended up working two jobs to support us.

At times I would get tired and frustrated with our situation and would talk to David. He told me sacrifices were reality and I needed to stop being so selfish. Soon a pattern developed. David would convince me I was the bad person, and then I would apologize hoping he would forgive me. It seemed when he wasn't sure what I was really thinking he would give me more attention and often surprises.

David's acts of kindness and devotion led to my greatest dream coming true, which was to own a horse. He had figured out how we could afford the horse and the board. I would work at the stable since I was an accomplished rider. The barn and horses became my passion and focus. I was in heaven thanks to David and spent every extra minute doing what I love to do. This made David jealous and he started to have outbursts.

Soon he had me quit my main job to find one that better suited his schedule. He prevented me from having my own life. He took our car away from me so I couldn't get to the barn and my horse. He wouldn't allow me to make friends or go out anywhere without him. When my mother or a friend called, he would hold me back away from the phone and tell them I wasn't there. The whole time David kept convincing me that I was the one at fault, that he was helping me and that I should be grateful that he still wanted to stay with me. I became so brainwashed that when he said we had to get married so I could prove my love for him, I believed that would give him assurance and life would be better.

Still with no job he insisted we go looking for the perfect engagement ring. David commissioned a diamond and designed the ring, which I paid for. With a ring on my finger the wedding plans became my mother's new project. She was planning a wedding that would be the event of the year among her friends. I started to feel that I had lost control of every area in my life. When I shared this with David he exploded.

I remember sobbing in a corner in our apartment thinking I could not go on like this anymore. I had two choices. I could end my life, or I could find the courage and strength to save my life. I got up off that floor, got into my car and drove back to Ontario. I left a note for David saying the engagement was off and that I was going home.

When I arrived at my parent's house, they were less than welcoming. I was immediately told the wedding invitations had been sent and that I was making a mess of everything. My mother's biggest concern was disappointing her guests, and my father was worried about getting back his deposits.

David's stepbrother John contacted me about three weeks after I got home. He was sympathetic and suggested we go fishing and get away for a day of relaxation. Boating, fishing, and the warm sun was just what I needed. John picked me up, and we went to a secluded island in the middle of a big lake. He asked me to jump out and grab the rope so we could dock and fish off the island. Once on shore, I realized what was going on. There with the blinding sun behind him was David. This had been a set up, and now I was trapped in the middle of the lake with David with nowhere to run.

Hours later David convinced me that I had to marry him because no one else would accept and love me the way he did. He made me feel that I should be grateful for his love and the sacrifice he was making for me. David insisted we go and tell my parents that the wedding was back on.

At the wedding, as I walked down the aisle, a voice in my head told me there was always suicide or divorce if things didn't work out.

We left for Alberta right after the wedding. Once alone with David the abuse started with more intensity since it had been building up inside him. The drive across Canada out to the west was the most frightening trip of my life.

Upon returning to our apartment in Edmonton David found a fulltime job, and he promised things would be better for us now that we were married. I desperately wanted to believe him and fall in love with the man who wrote me those amazing love letters so long ago. I made it my job to be the most devoted wife ever. It was the only way I would survive the nightmare I was living.

Life was good for a few weeks. It seemed David had changed for the better. Soon I became more relaxed and trusting, feeling guilty that I hadn't believed David when he said married life would be better for us.

Not long after our marriage, David came to me and told me it was time I got pregnant. The abuse grew, the threats got worse and the last thing I wanted was to bring a baby into this situation. I went for counseling to see what was wrong with me and to find the help I needed to be fixed. My therapist met me a few times and then was blunt enough to say the abuse would only get worse once a child was brought into the equation. It was suggested that David and I get counseling together.

David agreed to go only because he now had a chance to prove that I had all the problems. We sat for two hours with this woman therapist. David gave his side and painted himself as a most loving and best partner a girl could want. He suddenly also started talking therapist language, making reference to my dysfunctional upbringing and unresolved inner child issues. I was tongue-tied. How could I defend myself when he sounded so knowledgeable, sympathetic, and caring? In the end the therapist agreed that I was the one who needed help.

When we were in the parking lot outside of the therapist's office, David called me horrible things, and then picked me up and threw me over a car hood.

More counseling was recommended for both David and me. David would see a physiatrist on the assumption the doctor would help him deal with me. After three visits, I received a call from my own therapist who told me David had tried to punch his doctor. He had told David that he had sociopathic tendencies and a borderline personality. This meant I was in extreme danger. It was time to save myself.

I moved from place to place to hide from David, but he started to stalk me and threaten to kill my horse. The police were involved, but restraining orders back then weren't the best and David always found me. The police suggested I go back to Ontario, so I sold my horse and used the money to move back to Ontario, where I finally told my parents what had been going on.

One day shortly after my return home I saw a doctor about a rash. The doctor saw more than a rash and started asking me many questions. Two hours later I had broken down and told him everything including what my childhood had been like. Never had I faced this raw reality so openly and honestly with anyone before.

This doctor had me check into a live-in, 12-step program for adult children of alcoholics and co-dependants that very day. Dealing with addictions and all types of dependencies, breaking old patterns, building self-esteem, and self-confidence was a lifesaver for me.

It took courage and unwavering strength to face my past, recognize and accept the changes I had to make and learn to forgive others and myself. To this day I see the gifts this four-year period brought me because without this huge awakening I wouldn't have gotten the help I needed to become the person I am today. This time in my life has allowed me find and follow my life's purpose. It's my passion to help people defeat obstacles and limiting beliefs so they can feel the joy of empowerment and not be afraid to SHINE and live up to their true potential.

My story is not about a victim; it's about empowering change. Every negative in life is an opportunity to learn and grow for the better. All you have to do is believe this is true. The smallest positive is an assurance that you are capable and entitled to wonderful transformation.

About the Author

Cammie Ritchie lives in Ottawa, Canada. After university and college she explored various client service and entrepreneurial opportunities. She found her SHINE in real estate and performance and personal-growth coaching. Cammie is the owner and principal coach of ChangeIt! Coaching (www.changeitcoaching.com.) Cammie helps to move others toward their purpose and passion through awareness, growth, and action. Her success shows by the number of clients who have tripled their incomes, grown their businesses, and enhanced their lives. Email her at changitcoaching@gmail.com

The Bully's Gifts

Tina Dietz MS, NCC

"Everything can be taken from a man but one thing: the last of human freedoms – to choose one's attitude in any given set of circumstances, to choose one's own way."
—Viktor Frankl

The top of the jungle gym was the only safe place on the playground I could find. Well, fairly safe. I stare at the sky, waiting for recess to be over. Okay, there are three teachers watching, so it should be safe to come down now. There's only a little time left before the bell rings, so I try to hurry. I'm not much of a climber, especially now that my tummy is getting in the way. I feel so slow, so heavy reaching my foot down for the next rung of the slippery metal structure, but eating is the only thing that fills up the hole where I'm always scared. At least it does for a little while.

I walk just as fast as I can past the slide towards the gym doors, but I didn't see them coming down the slide and now it's too late. I'm surrounded and the pit inside me opens up wide enough to swallow me whole. I can't let them know I'm scared, I can't. If I cry, I might never be able to stop. But now I'm surrounded. I'm surrounded and the teachers are too far away to see that this isn't a playground game. Not for me. Why are they doing this? Why do they hate me so much?

I try to say something tough, to brush it off and get out of the circle, but Kevin steps forward. It feels like he's towering over me. "Jeff," he calls to one of his so called lieutenants—"Get her."

He punches me twice in the stomach before I manage to scream loud enough to startle him and break through the circle. I stumble towards the teachers, crying. I don't know if I can survive second grade.

Remember back when you were a kid and kids would tease each other that someone had "cooties?" We didn't have cooties in my second grade, we had "Tina Germs." This social movement was started by one boy in my class who had decided that somehow I was his enemy. His name was Kevin. We were in class all day together and we also rode the same bus, so my mornings and afternoons outside of school were spent waiting for the other shoe to drop. There was no safe haven, not anywhere. I have to give him points for being thorough—he managed to get the whole class in on it. He even developed a military structure among his friends to target me as the enemy on the playground.

Boys will, after all, be boys, right?

The teachers saw no reason to interfere with a screaming, jeering circle of kids surrounding one small girl—right?

"She's just mature for her age so the other kids have a hard time relating to her," the school counselor told my parents when I asked them for help. "Don't worry, they'll catch up with her eventually."

My parents had no real reason to worry, no reason to question the explanation of a professional, certainly not on the word of a second grader-- right?

I was an only child and academically "gifted," which meant that I was often separated from the rest of the class. Socially, I was awkward. On top of the "Tina Germs" thing that the boys started, with the girls I got teased for using "big words" and being bossy. I'm sure I must've acted pretty desperate at the time, looking for some kind of foothold, someone I could play with and talk to. My parents worked pretty much all the time in the family business we lived upstairs from, so mostly I was by myself at home too. I got myself up in the morning; I spent time by myself in the afternoon. I knew my parents loved me, they just were busy and I didn't want to bother them. So I ate. It didn't really matter what I ate, it just needed to fill me up so I didn't feel like I was going to die of loneliness. I remember thinking that food is what held me together. It dulled the fear and sadness so that I could put on a good face and keep my dad from being upset that his daughter seemed so "miserable" all the time. As part of my quest to fill myself up, that year I learned how to bake.

My birthday came in May, and I was damn proud of those cupcakes. Chocolate cake, chocolate frosting, and a little marshmallow face on every one . . . I made sure each face was different. Second grade had been rough, but it was MY DAY. Birthdays are sacred ground when you're 8 years old.

Kevin, of course, doesn't look at me when I put his cupcake on his desk, but I expect that. At least he doesn't whisper some nasty name. I realize I've been holding my breath as I walk by him, and suddenly gulp for air.

And then it's time. Mrs. C motions for me to stand in the front of the class, and she begins the Happy Birthday song . . . but the 25 pairs of eyes in front of me are indifferent, their voices horribly silent. And I finally break, because I have nothing left to lose.

The whole story of the year pours out of me, all jumbled between sobs and snot and I can't stop myself, I don't even know what I'm saying but I do know that it's shocking the crap out of the entire room because there's no sound except for my hysterical tirade. Mrs. C turns red, Kevin turns white, and the whole class just stares at the 3 of us.

That's when the miracle happens. In response to what feels like me dissolving into a puddle of goo on the floor, all it takes to stop what has been a year of isolation and torture is one 90 second conversation between Mrs. C and Kevin. Less than 2 minutes.

In one crazy birthday moment towards the end of that school year, it finally all stopped. From Kevin, at least.

The bullying was never that bad again, but once a child is branded as a target it's very difficult to get that label changed. It was like a pack mentality where I was academically the alpha, but socially the lone wolf. Believe me, I really could've done without being the only kid in class who didn't get valentines in 3rd grade. Or being cornered on the playground by a group of 5th graders (several of whom were supposedly friends) chanting "chubbles" at me, or having my 6th grade yearbook come back signed from a couple of boys with "BUTTERBALL" written in big letters over my picture. In 8th grade, every time I went to sit down in English class the boy behind me would look at me and say "fat," even though I wasn't anymore. I'm sure you can imagine the treacherous waters I struggled to navigate in High School.

I first found my personal source of unwavering strength in books. Books were my joy, my escape, my hope. If the characters in the books I read could overcome problems way bigger than name calling and isolation, why not me too? So I kept trying, kept speaking up, kept putting myself forward. Besides, I had already had a meltdown in front of everyone so what could be worse than that? Somewhere inside me, long before a friend convinced me to read Viktor Frankel's work, I reached for that last of human freedoms—the freedom to choose my response. I found within myself the desire to be better, do better, and make my struggles count for something. I also found myself captivated by curiosity: what would make people do such crappy things? These core passions have shaped my life. My curiosity led to my first psychology class in high school, then to my first women's retreat, and into a whole new world of understanding and empowerment which opened up for me as a result. Being at the receiving end of the bad school counseling in second grade led me to appreciate the difference when, in seventh grade, I experienced good family counseling with my parents. This in turn led me to put myself into individual counseling when I turned 16 a few years later. I had always been a good student and I approached therapy the same way. I did the work, and things began to shift in me.

Years later, when I was 27, I hosted a party for a bunch of people I had known since high school. I was working as a school counselor and developing a teen leadership center, which is probably not surprising. I was married, I had gone to graduate school to become a therapist, I had friends, and I was living my life.

At the end of the party, Kevin, who had married a good friend of mine, presses an envelope into my hand and tells me to read it after the party. It's an apology letter for what he did in the 2nd grade.

In the letter he shares with me that his pastor had recently delivered a sermon asking the congregation to look into their lives and see if there was anyone in their past from whom they needed to ask forgiveness. Kevin remembered what had happened with me in second grade, and now he tells me how sorry he is, how he can't imagine what he would do if he saw anyone do to one of his children what he had done to me. He had become a middle school teacher and he assures me in the letter that he will make certain that children don't get bullied in his classroom.

Ironically, he immediately speculates that I probably barely remember what happened . . . because clearly I'm doing so well, I must have gotten past it . . . right?

He doesn't know I'm giving this party at the advice of my therapist who has been treating me for PTSD symptoms which re-emerged when I started working with children in the schools. He certainly doesn't know that the reason I specifically invited him and his wife is that I had already forgiven him. I had forgiven them all, and this party is an act of completion and love out of that forgiveness.

As I finished reading his letter, I realized the nature of the Gift I had chosen to harvest from the seeds of the bullying. I had come to know that I always have the freedom to choose my response, to find meaning in the pain and make it count.

These days I feel compassion for those who bullied me, and even gratitude for the crucible from which I emerged with unwavering strength. However, that didn't happen overnight. The hurt child I was still surfaces sometimes, and my adult self takes her by the hand and reminds her that she is safe. Healing takes work, growth takes time, and if we want to thrive we have to be diligent and compassionate gardeners of our own growth.

Sometimes I get asked why I forgave those people who hurt me, but why would I poison myself with that bitterness when I could choose to free myself by granting forgiveness? The most valuable gifts I have ever given myself are the ones which involved investing in my own personal development, whether that development was education, therapy, energy work, spiritual exploration or allowing contribution from others. These are the training tools I use to keep developing inner muscles, habits, and capacities to step beyond my past and create the life I want. Since I can't change the past, I might as well use those painful experiences and lessons in ways that make a difference rather than hold me back. I claimed my freedom to choose my response, and I continue to choose to be powerful and loving rather than frozen in fear.

About the Author

Tina Dietz MS, NCC lives in nifty places like Costa Rica, Florida, and New York with her husband and two very bouncy kids. She is an internationally acclaimed business coach and speaker on a mission to cause 10,000 thriving businesses. Tina primarily works with business owners who want to make a great living and have awesome lives doing what they absolutely love. She has been featured on ABC and in Massage & Bodywork magazine, Massage Today, Feminine Soul Magazine and around the radio dial on shows like the Million Dollar Mindset Show, Money for Lunch, and The Great Metamorphosis. Visit http://www.thisistinadietz.com to learn more.

Embracing the Gift

Dr Terry A. Gordon

"It is the falls of our life that provide us with the energy to propel us to a much higher level."
—The Kabbalah

Crap happens! We all know that. Why it happens has confounded some of the wisest people who have walked this earth. The question of why bad things happen to innocent people is even more perplexing.

I first encountered this dilemma as a young man when my father suffered a painfully, horrific death due to prostate cancer. Dad was a prince among men and from my perspective as a 22 year-old, I couldn't come to grips as to why a good God would allow a gentle man to suffer in such an inhumane fashion. It would take me decades of searching before I stumbled upon a clear understanding.

All too often when confronted with adversity, we tend to blame someone or something else for our misfortune. God might become the recipient of that displeasure. If not the one being blamed, often we ascribe harsh conditions in our lives to "God's will." Some believe that God punishes us for evil deeds we have committed in the past and that we deserve the heartache that comes our way. I do not personally subscribe to that conviction.

Carl Perkins once said, "If it weren't for the rocks in its bed, the stream would have no song." Such is the effect of obstacles in our path. They actually enrich the experience.

I would learn this painful lesson through a horrific family tragedy of immense proportions, a resolve-weakening event that forced me to re-think everything.

It was June 2009 and life was great. I had been retired from my cardiology practice for over a year anticipating with my wife, Angela, the many exciting things life had in stored for us. Our three daughters, Mattie-Rose, Laila, and Britt had graduated from college with degrees in education; our son, Tyler, had just completed his sophomore year studying business at Fort Lewis College in Durango, Colorado.

Just when we thought we had it all figured out, life, as we knew it imploded. In the early morning hours of June 30th, I received one of the worst phone calls a parent could imagine. The grave voice on the other end of the line informed me that our son, Tyler, had been involved in a near fatal car crash in which he had shattered his neck. The result was a severe spinal cord injury. And then came the dreaded words . . . "Your son is quadriplegic."

In a nanosecond, everything changed.

A Life-Flight helicopter had been dispatched to Durango to pick up its precious cargo. Tyler was to be transferred to Swedish Medical Center in Denver where he would undergo emergency surgery to stabilize his fractured neck and hopefully prevent any further spinal cord damage.

Within an hour of receiving the devastating news, I had hastily packed a bag, bolted from our home, and was speeding up to the Cleveland airport trying to get on the next non-stop flight to Denver. I had to see my son before they took in him into surgery. I needed to tell him how much I loved him.

Somehow I was able to board an overbooked flight and get settled into my seat for the longest flight of my life. Now incommunicado for three nerve-wracking hours, I was like a caged cat. I didn't know if Tyler was alive or dead, brain-damaged or bleeding from internal organ damage. My mind was in total chaos with excruciatingly painful thoughts banging around inside my skull.

I began praying deeper than I had ever prayed before. I pleaded, Please God; help me get to Denver in time. Help me help my son. Help me help my family. Help me be strong. Help me. . . . Help!

It felt like I was caught in a tornado. It was loud and whooshing, and dank. I looked down into the funnel of the tornado and it was pure blackness. The loud rush of the cold wind was deafening. It was the most frightening experience of my life. God, please help me. I ask this not for myself, but for those I love.

As I was sucked deeper into the funnel, the same thought kept scrolling through my mind over and over again, I can't do this. I can't do this.

Gradually the loud whooshing sound began to abate as the darkened dankness dissolved. I was slowly being enveloped strand by strand in a cocoon of white noise. It became this place of unfathomable peace, yet I was still repeating the words, I can't do this, I can't. It was then that I felt the Presence. I don't recall if I actually heard God's voice or if I perceived the words from deep within, but the meaning was clear when God said, "Know that there are no mistakes. Everything is in perfect order . . . even this."

I remember questioning whether I had the strength to endure this storm; I doubted if I could lead my family through this calamity.

God's answer was clear: "You can do this."

But, dear God, how? Help me please.

The path became clear when God offered the most profound advice: "Treat this as if you had chosen it to be."

I pondered the thought as if I had chosen it to be.

Now, why would I choose a tragedy such as this?

What possible good could come from such a life-altering calamity? What lessons could possibly be hidden within such turmoil?

I have since come to understand that life has a way of offering us precisely what we need the most. Many of the world's religions promote the notion that what is to be experienced in one's lifetime is chosen and predestined prior to birth. This is either divinely determined or as some believe, the actual selection is made by the individual who chooses ahead of time what is to be learned during a particular lifetime. In either case, the impetus behind the choice is predicated on the spiritual needs of that individual.

For me, the epiphany crystallized once I acknowledged that anything that happens simply couldn't be a mistake —because it has been chosen. I came to appreciate there is no such thing as an accident or a misstep; everything is in perfect order . . . even Tyler's horrific injury!

As I began navigating this tumultuous storm in our lives, the challenge for me became adjusting my perception of these events enough to recognize the presence of God within them. And in order to do that, I had to look beyond what my mind wanted to judge as good or bad.

Despite this understanding, it is impossible for me to convey in words the immense, overpowering sorrow this father experiences watching his son endure such an ocean of suffering. But it was while weathering this horrific upheaval that I began to catch glimpses of the paradoxically positive blessings hidden within what I had initially perceived as one of the worst "tragedies" imaginable.

Most of us think in terms of duality, that there exist two extremes. There's hot and there's cold. There's good and there's bad. What I've come to appreciate is that the human realm in which we find ourselves is the perfect circumstance in which we can find what it is we all seek, insight. None of us is immune to the pain and turmoil of this existence. But life is perfectly balanced, not only with those things that cause us to suffer, it is beautifully coupled with those things that bring us pleasure as well. And because of that, we're not overly burdened with the negative aspects of these experiences.

The question becomes . . . is there such a thing as a negative experience? I don't think so.

I have discovered that these so-called "negative" experiences can actually be blessings in disguise; they can become the catalyst for change, fodder for growth. The challenge is that we must free ourselves of attachment to what we perceive as good experiences as much as we must learn let go of the aversion to those events we consider negative.

In life, there is no duality. The monsoon is countered by a calm, sunny day; perfect health is balanced by life-threatening disease and injury; darkness by illumination. These perceived opposites are in truth conjoined with one another; they are one in the same. This is the paradoxical unity described by Lao Tzu as related in the 2nd verse of the Tao Te Ching:

"Under heaven all can see beauty as beauty, only because there is ugliness. All can know good, as good only because there is evil. The difficult is born in the easy. Long is defined by short, the high by the low."

Nothing can protect us from experiencing our share of dark days. We will all have them. But we can do something to transform so-called calamities into opportunities for growth, enlightenment, and positive change. After all, our life experiences become calamities only if we make the conscious decision to make tragedies out of them.

The difficult days I experienced became the driving force of change. Rather than lamenting adversity, I chose to be grateful for it. I embraced and accepted it as a gift from the Divine, a marvelous learning tool. This gift certainly didn't come enveloped in beautiful wrapping paper. Its package was so hideous that initially, it was unimaginable what possible benefit could come from it.

But the gift I received offered me a new lens through which to view life's experiences. It showed me a new way to interpret adversity, a way that ultimately helped propel me to a place of much higher consciousness. Within this gift were lessons that helped promote my spiritual development and maturation in ways I could never have anticipated. It has had the same impact on our son, Tyler as well.

By learning to be grateful for the adversity, I began seeing it as an opportunity to transform turmoil, disappointment, and suffering into understanding, insight, and resolve.

Ultimately, I discovered that I had one of two choices how to respond to this perceived nightmare. At first I tried to resist the gift and in doing so, became a victim of this tragic event. But I quickly discovered the more I resisted, the greater magnified the pain and suffering became.

Resistance led to resentment. Resentment fueled anger, while intensifying the turmoil and fear.

The other choice I had was to accept the offering for what it was, a magnanimous gift from God that would teach me everything I possibly could learn from it.

It was only when I allowed myself to change the thought that meaning began trickling into my consciousness. Peace ensued and my transformative enlightenment began expanding as an unwavering strength enveloped my soul. With this unwavering strength came a knowing that I could handle whatever "gifts" might be sent my way.

My journey had brought me to a crossroad. Rather than continue on the same familiar path I had walked for years, I chose a new way of interpreting adversity. A gift had been offered. Placed before me was a tool I could use to transform suffering into insight. I didn't quite understand it, but I felt a strange sense that I had just been blessed.

The wisdom from the ancient mystical text of Judaism called the Kabbalah has forever reshaped my understanding of life: "It is the falls of our life that provide us with the energy to propel us to a much higher level."

We must learn not to resist the falls of our life, but to embrace them. Because they offer us the milieu to transform, giving us the springboard to transcend to the place of higher consciousness where growth, enlightenment and yes, complete healing occur.

We should be grateful for the falls of our lives . . . .

Namaste

About the Author

Dr. Terry A. Gordon, Hay House author of No Storm Lasts Forever graduated with a degree in Psychology from Emory University. A Cleveland Clinic trained cardiologist, Terry is nationally known in matters of the heart. In 2002 he was named The American Heart Association National Physician of the Year for his tireless work helping to save the lives of our most precious resource, our children, placing Automated External Defibrillators (AEDs) in over 4,470 schools in Ohio. As a direct result, more than 15 lives have been saved. Now retired from the practice of Cardiology, Terry's purposeful life is to continue mending hearts by sharing with others his insight to what we all desire . . . Peace, Shalom, and Salaam. Visit http://www.drterrygordon.com

Loss to Laughter

Annie Spalding

"I sought my soul,
But my soul I could not see.
I sought my God,
But my God eluded me.
I sought my brother,
And I found all three."
—Author Unknown

My brother John was diagnosed at age 29 with Stage 4 colon cancer. That same year, my marriage of six years dissolved around me. The evening John passed away, I sat in my car wondering which parking lot I could sleep in. I had just moved back to my hometown, and it was as if I were a stranger. All I had worked towards in my life was stripped away. My older brother was gone. The proud feeling of being married and owning my home was gone. Having my own bed to sleep in was gone. I was incredibly lost in a maze of confusion and no longer knew who I was or why I was even alive. Throughout all of this turmoil, I never imagined that being at my brother's bedside would give me the gift to build something new and good in my life.

John, with his unwavering strength, surpassed the six month mark he was given and went on to battle his cancer for four years. These four years included 85 chemo treatments, multiple surgeries, detox from pain medications (He maxed out very quickly from the undulating intensity of his pain.), and the creation of his music album he titled Loveland, The Beautiful Truth.

"Well," as he would casually say, "that is where I'm going so, I'll name it Loveland."

According to his hospice nurse, he had a stronger will to live than anyone she had ever worked with in her 20 years of service.

John brought love and an endless ability to give to anyone who came in contact with him. At our brother Steve's wedding, a homeless man came up to John and asked if my brother would give him some money. John, who had no cash at the time, realized that this man needed not just money but love, attention, and warmth. John then took his tuxedo coat off, gave this man his undershirt, and shook his hand with the utmost respect. That is who John was to all.

In August, four months before he passed away, I experienced a battle of my own. I was going through a confusing and shocking divorce. John was the only one I could not tell over the phone that my marriage dissolved. I purchased a flight back to Seattle to find myself sitting on his overused wooden chair. He sat across from me on his couch with his tattered blue jeans, white t-shirt, and usual disheveled hair. His concerned yet loving eyes were looking in my direction.

"Hmm, something's up," his words quickly came out. "What's going on, Annie?"

I explained to John the mess I was in. How I was heartbroken, not just because of the hurt feelings I had, but I also did not want to take any attention away from John, attention he needed to get through his battle.

John laid his head back on his couch with his chin pointed up towards the sky.

"Annie, I can die in peace now that you finally found the courage to leave and move towards a healthier life." He said with a deep sigh. "And, as for the attention, it will be fantastic that you will have to answer all the sad questions now."

We instantly released the pressure of discussing divorce and the dying process, and just laughed. Within a month I had packed my few belongings from my home in Colorado and had driven from Denver to Seattle.

As John's cancer spread to his lungs, liver, and lymph nodes, his energy began to drop. He had no eyelashes or eyebrows. The skin on his cheeks was so close to his facial bones I could see the outline of his skull. Panic attacks were increasing. He felt as though he couldn't breathe and was on oxygen and a morphine pump constantly. I often placed a chair in the center of the living room on his way towards the bathroom so he had a place to rest during the ten steps it took to get to his bathroom.

September rolled around and even John admitted his body was deteriorating faster than his will and ambition could keep up with. In the car one day, my mother asked him how he was feeling.

"Mom, I feel like dust in the wind." He replied.

My mother quietly took in a deep breath and slowed the car down as her eyes welled with tears. Her heart was broken. He asked my mom the ultimate question, "Mom, would you ask dad if he would make my cremation box?"

She was speechless. My mother fell numb to the question, the thought and the reality of what was happening, but the words came out, "Yes, of course I will ask him for you, John."

The following day I was at my parents' home and asked my father, a hobby woodworker, how he felt about John's request.

He replied without hesitation, "Annie, I was honored to be asked." He sat next to me and continued, "Honey, what I realized this morning as I was looking in the garage for the right piece of wood, was that in the rafters, I have had a piece of Alaskan cedar since the exact year John was born. I never knew what I was going to do with it. The answer has been given to me."

For the next six weeks I watched my father measure, cut, and sand the pristine wood while he tried out different inlays and asked which one I liked best. He designed the perimeter to measure exactly 33 inches, the same age John was when he passed. The cross he carved for the top was 7 x 5 inches. John was born in '75. This was the most difficult, yet most beautiful experience I could've imagined would come through my father. To know that my dad raised his son to live a life of joy and steady direction made it very difficult to watch him, piece by piece, designing the wooden box that his first-born son's ashes would rest in. He stood tall during the entire process of creating his most honorable, selfless piece of woodworking.

The last few days before John's passing were filled with both love and chaos. John's home was bursting at the seams with every one of his friends and family surrounding him. His deepest wishes were being met.

On November 23, 2008 John's pain was so great that he was given a drug that put him into a coma. Deep within, I felt he could hear and understand, but he was unable to respond to anything. An hour before my brother passed away, I sat next to him holding his hand. I talked to him, letting him know where everyone was in the house.

"Mom and dad are sitting on the couch reading. Steve and Tatum are taking a nap." I explained.

As I continued talking, John began moving his mouth and revealing his teeth. I was shocked! I became frantic, trying very hard to ask questions to see what he wanted.

"John, what do you want?" I asked. "Can I get you some ice chips? Do you want mom or dad? Do you need another blanket?"

My mind raced to figure out what he could possibly need. Finally, looking at that toothy grin, it came to me.

We had this long running joke that always made us laugh. Because I am a dental hygienist, John bragged about his own teeth to me all the time. He would always hysterically joke around that he wanted a certain phrase written on his headstone.

I stopped with my serious questions, and in the same tone of sarcasm we always used I said, "I know what you really want, John! You want me to make sure you have 'Age 33 with No Cavities' written on your headstone!"

I didn't even think that he could move, but after I repeated our joke his head slowly moved back. He mustered up all his energy and smiled ear to ear. He very deliberately pursed his lips. I gently took the oxygen mask off and gave him one last kiss goodbye.

He gave me the greatest gift possible: a final laugh together!

The moment John passed; my mom and I looked one another in the eye, felt it and said these words to each other, "Life is all about one thing. LOVE."

The most tragic experiences I saw as my brother slowly moved from this world to the next ironically granted me the greatest gift possible: an opportunity to look at our lives in a whole new way. I can see the depth of others' life struggles with great empathy, compassion, and power. I can also feel the valley of sadness in others and know with every part of me that there is a mountain of joy coming their way, if they choose it.

I have created a business that educates and assists others passing through tragic circumstances, helping them to find new and joyful lives. We must accept the duality of life: good and bad, right and wrong, up and down, sadness and joy, loss and life.

The key is making the choice to find the good within the maze of confusion. Laughter, light, and love will reveal themselves at the right time. My brother taught me that we can only create new growth in our own lives when we dare to let go of that which no longer serves our situation.

About the Author

Annie Spalding resides in her hometown of Seattle, WA. She has practiced dental hygiene. She and her mother have survived cancer, but Annie has lost her brother, grandmother, and grandfather to the disease. Annie has created a business to assist others transcend their grief, loss, and sadness. She helps clients dig deep and use their experiences to transform their lives to worlds filled with joy, happiness, and balance, just as she has done. Learn more about her work at anniespalding.com. She has also started a movement and business in recycling plastic in dental offices, you can read more about this effort at cleanseaconsulting.com.

Matters of My Heart: True GRITT

Willie Tart

"Heroes are never perfect, but they're brave, they're authentic, they're courageous, determined, discreet, and they've got grit."
—Wade Davis

'm no hero. I believed I was doomed from the start. I had been born prematurely, and the doctors only expected me to live for a few precious minutes. I was always a slow reader and didn't understand hard math problems, and in elementary school I was diagnosed with a learning disability.

Luckily, my parents would have none of it. They rejected governmental assistance and flat out refused to accept that I was a limited person in any way. They helped me work through challenges and taught me true GRITT. GRITT stands for Godly Resolve in Troubled Times. Without true GRITT and my parents' support, I could never have earned my high school diploma, associate's degree, Bachelor of Science, or the master's degree that I will soon complete.

In my early life I relied on my parents a lot, and my dependency planted a tiny seed of fear in my mind. I never believed I could be successful without them. What if something happened to them? What would I do? I feared losing them even more than I did dying myself!

As I matured, the small seed of dependency took root in my heart and grew into a deep fear about losing anyone I loved.

Fear is a primal emotion and brings out different emotions in different people. When fear is present, you see the good, the bad, and the ugly emerge from the most unexpected places. It is when we are afraid that we learn to rely

54

not on our earthy support, but on our Creator and the unwavering strength that comes from Him.

In recent years, I experienced three distinct opportunities to practice letting go and relying on God.

Tabitha: My Heart, My Lover, My Best Friend, My Wife, My Queen

I was assigned to Lackland Air Force Base in San Antonio, Texas. I was the newly appointed Command Operations Supervisor working nights. This role carried a lot of responsibilities including working as a trauma team member, becoming the public affairs representative, and acting as a first line of contact should anyone pass away for any reason. This meant I was responsible for notifying the family should any member of our unit not survive.

About a week into the post, I received my first such assignment. One of our own had died as a result of a pulmonary embolism. That means that a large blood clot had lodged in one of the main arteries of the lungs, completely cutting off blood flow and causing sudden death. The doctor and I had to break the bad news to the victim's spouse, and I will always associate grief with that experience.

Not even a month later, my wife Tabitha, who had been traveling a lot with her job, started feeling very run down. We thought she might have a severe cold or pneumonia, and she went to the emergency room for help. They tried treating her symptoms, but finally on the third trip, a trauma team member ordered a chest x-ray. The test revealed that Tabitha also had a pulmonary embolism!

I felt as though my soul was being torn apart! I was devastated and so afraid I would lose my wonderful wife that I could hardly pray. My pastor, family, friends, and the duty chaplain all reminded me to practice true GRITT during that frightening day.

The next day we learned that the brilliant physician's assistant who had ordered the test had saved Tabitha's life. We had caught it in time, and the clot could be treated.

A wave of blessed relief washed over me, and I thanked God for seeing us through the scariest night of my life! I am grateful to this day for that one P.A. who had been cautious and made such a difference in all our lives.

Jaquan: My Heart, My Prince, My Son

In 1998 my wife's only sister passed away. Her son Jaquan, only nine years old at the time, told us that his mother had gone to be with the Lord, which he said was OK because she wasn't suffering any longer. He said she was at peace.

We were astonished at his maturity and comforted by his faith. We grew so close that Tabitha and I decided to adopt Jaquan, making him our own amazing son.

A few years after Tabitha's diagnosis, she and Jaquan went to live with her family in the Pacific Northwest during the school year. I was stationed in North Carolina and talked to them every day.

One night Tabitha said Jaquan had not been feeling well. Shortly afterward he collapsed at school and had to be taken to the emergency room. He was suffering from kidney failure, and my fear for his life brought me to my knees.

I was devastated that the fourteen-year-old boy I loved so dearly could experience such a terrible disease. What made it even worse was that I could not get there to be with him!

I packed up everything and began applying for a special needs assignment. As I awaited my new assignment, I had myself tested to see if I was a match and could donate a kidney to help Jaquan. It was a happy day when I learned I was a 100% match and could absolutely help alleviate my son's suffering!

Months passed. My application for a special assignment was denied twice, and my hope faded. My parents and church family were there again, reminding me to stay faithful and that God was working His plan.

Finally, on the third try, my application was approved! I was going to be with Tabitha and Jaquan. I would move, donate a kidney to Jaquan, and he would be OK!

Shortly before I was scheduled to leave, I had a minor sinus procedure to ensure I was in tiptop shape for the organ transplant. In recovery, I had a serious reaction, and subsequently several blood tests were run. In the midst of all this chaos, my doctors discovered I had diabetes.

"Well, that's OK, right?" I asked them. "You can treat that with diet and medication these days, can't you?"

They confirmed that I wasn't in any danger and could easily be treated and maintain an active, healthy life. The devastation came when they explained that I would not be able to donate my kidney to my son. Diabetes is one of the few conditions that prevents one from donating organs.

I begged and pleaded with many healthcare providers, but no one would authorize an exception. I was completely tormented knowing that I was the only person who could have helped Jaquan, but now he would continue his painful suffering because I no longer met donor criteria.

He continues his struggle against kidney disease today, and I still fight against fate wishing I could give him my organ. Family and friends keep me going. They remind me every day that our greatest pains are sources of our greatest blessings.

I am charged to live with true GRITT and trust God with my son.

Dad: My Heart, My Leader, My Mentor, My Inspiration

I regularly attend classes to maintain my certifications, and one summer I took a course to renew my CPR certification. This class was different from the sessions I had taken in the past because they spent way more time helping us observe and identify the signs of a heart attack.

Later that fall, I was staying with my parents near my base, while Jaquan and Tabitha stayed with her family out West.

I loved staying with my parents. Their relationship was such a perfect model for me, so full of love for each other and the Lord. My dad actually taught me what real love in a relationship is. When I was quite young, my mom was struck by lightning. My dad grabbed her hand, and I was terrified that I was about to lose both my parents. But in the instant they joined hands, my dad yelled, "Jesus!" and an immediate calm filled the air. I felt like I witnessed a miracle and that the power of my dad's love saved my mom that day.

But during this particular fall, I had been working for months without a single day off. I needed a day of rest and asked my supervisor if I could take off the next day. He agreed, and I was excited to be able to rest and relax at home.

I slept a little late, ate a leisurely breakfast, and had gone back to my room to tidy up. I had only been back there a short time when my mother knocked on my door and told me something was wrong with my dad.

I walked out and knew what was happening as soon as I saw him. He came towards me and collapsed in my arms.

I went into military mode and instructed my mom to get the phone, go out to the porch, and call 911.

She looked confused and asked, "Why go out to the porch?"

"So the medics can see you when they drive up!" I exclaimed. In truth, I didn't want her to see me performing CPR on my dad.

I carried him to the living room and began pumping his heart and breathing for him. He came around just as the paramedics arrived.

True GRITT during this emergency had been built since my childhood, and I knew that my dad loved my mom and me and that he was powerfully connected to God. I am grateful every single day that he survived and is still doing well today.

When we live in fear, I believe God presents us with opportunities to overcome it. He will give us chance after chance to learn to let go of our earthly dependencies and trust in Him. These three significant life events have shown me that I must cherish my relationships, but that I cannot depend on them for my own existence.

I am no hero and have faced many more personal challenges. But with all of these obstacles, I always had people around me to remind me to rely on God and His infinite wisdom.

My parents have always encouraged me and planted in me a faith that has helped me overcome, move forward, and accomplish my divine purpose. I have lived a life of true GRITT, and I have learned that trusting God is the only way to live through fearful times. He blesses us with his saints, and whenever he calls them back, we can be sure they are at peace. True GRITT helps us thank Him for the time we had and the lessons we learned.

About the Author

Willie Tart serves our country in the Navy, Coast Guard and Marines as a clinical information systems trainer, teaching healthcare providers how to maximize quality of care using Electronic Medical Record, served over 20 years in the USAF, and as serve as clergy on the Ecclesiastical leadership at the Maranatha Family Worship Center for over 10 years. His true GRITT helped him overcome failures, hurt and challenges. He uses the power of love to help others live in true GRITT, trusting God and letting go of earthly dependencies. Connect with Willie and Tabitha on Facebook. They share an account called "Willie Tabitha Tart" and page named "Matters of My Soul: A Heartfelt Legacy" www.facebook.com/MattersOfMySoul. His upcoming release The Legacy of My Soul: True GRITT-Godly Resolve in Trying Times will be released this fall. Updates will be on his Facebook page.

Forgiveness

Jeanne Henning

"The best way to deal with the ebb and flow of life is to be grateful for your experience and treasure what you still have. Being grateful enables us to accept what is, see other possibilities, and overcome the grief so we can get out of being stuck in a non-productive state and move on."
—Excerpt from: "If I Loved You, What Would I Tell You?"

I had been wandering around Europe for four months and wanted to be home for my birthday. I stayed with my parents for a couple of weeks, where my things were stored. I worked out where I wanted to live for a while—Santa Barbara. I arrange to get a job in the hospital's ICU as a registered nurse. It had been my practice to work a while, save my money and then travel. Later I would find a job elsewhere.

My father had been having intermittent chest pain and had been sent to San Francisco to see a specialist. There were no procedures planned and he seemed to be his usual robust self. He was working at his job operating a crane taking logs off of trucks and putting them in huge high piles. It was fun to watch him work, he was like an artist.

About a month later I was living in the nurse's residence at the hospital when I got THE CALL. My sister said "Dad is dead." My world would never be the same.

It was surreal at the funeral to see his friends and coworkers there. I kept thinking, "I will have to tell Dad about them." I was not accepting what was. I think we all experience that sort of denial when the reality is too painful to accept. I realized after hearing comments that the chest pain had worsened and there was nothing medical science experts could do. He had waited until I got home from Europe to die because he knew I would be deeply affected.

Our relationship was unusual because of his family history. His father had run away from home in Germany because his own father had an uncontrollable temper and beat his children. He worked on a ship to come to the USA, he married and had children. He also became a beater. My father swore on his father's grave he would NEVER do that. One day, though, he did beat me, I was 9. I didn't know what I had done wrong but I knew I must never be a bad little girl.

He told me the next day he would never spank me again and he never did. It changed him, the guilt was incredible and he kept his distance from me. I felt I was unlovable. I was afraid of him and he could easily see that and it destroyed a part of him. Ultimately, over the years, it would cause his early death of "broken" heart disease.

I felt, at his death, "Now I will never be able to be loved by him. It was impossible, he was gone." What I didn't realize was he loved me and adored who I was—a little fairy child who loved to dance and twirl and sing my little songs. That he had hurt that precious little one was more than he could bear.

When I was older and found out about the family history from other relatives I was able to piece together what had actually happened. It was nothing at all to do with me. I had taken it personally and was able to see he was a victim the same way I was. I realized there was nothing to forgive.

I had sublimated his death and now needed to pull it all back out and go through the grieving process. I was able to see beyond the one incident and realized he really did love me.

It has been a journey of self-realization because I felt unworthy of love and unlovable. Not only did I need to cope with his death but go through the old experiences and see how I had misinterpreted them as they happened. When I looked at them from the new perspective it was easily apparent I got things wrong. I had inadvertently made his life difficult in ways I could not know at the time—my obvious fear of him. It is human nature as a child, of course, but I now have compassion for a fellow victim.

When you are able to look at painful old stories from your past and find the truth hidden there it releases their hold on you, and they do have a hold on you whether you realize it or not. When we are young we are hungry for knowledge and absorb everything we can, not realizing we may not interpret what we find correctly. Those were covered by more stories but the deep one being incorrect meant the rest were tainted. Our subconscious mind feeds these experiences to us to help us make new decision and find our way through life. When the information is incorrect it can cause us more problems. When they surface and you look at them and see if they were wrongly interpreted and clear the input from your subconscious also changes. It is important to do this clearing. It is not just coping; it is changing your perspective that enhances your entire life. Changing what is—he died—cannot be done but understanding what really went on enables one to be able to move on without the suffering some have to go through with unresolved issues. Few people go through life without issues that need to be resolved. Some try to sublimate, hide the issues and "forget," but they remain in our subconscious and affect us anyway.

Although I did not work through the grief and loss at the time of his death, it was a lingering suffering just below the surface of my consciousness. I definitely was affected but just did not know the source because I wouldn't let myself think about it. At that time in my life I made decisions that ultimately were not in my best interest. We all do that to one degree or another because our focus is on what has been lost and we want to replace it. We don't always consider that some things cannot be replaced. We must carve out a new way of viewing life and have new choices, not try to recreate the past.

When these things happen we need to realize we are vulnerable and not make major decisions right then. It is likely we will not be making wise choices that are far-reaching, we are immersed in loss and grasping for what seems familiar, not what is best ultimately.

There will come a time when we are able to move on but some will choose to stay in that abyss of grief and sorrow. Realizing life goes on and we are still alive is what to reach for; when you can reach for that you are able to move on. No one can predict how long it will take to get to that point because everyone handles these experiences differently. Just do the best you can, where you are, with what you have to work with.

Self-care is important during this time because our focus is elsewhere and we neglect to realize we are hurting and need to provide for our needs and treat ourselves gently and kindly, as we would another person. Tender loving care is needed because you are precious still even though it may seem your world has collapsed around you. You will get through this—if it is your intent.

Being out in nature can be very healing because you will see the sun is still shining, the birds still sing and flowers still grow. Being able to notice these things can give you a needed respite from your thoughts. It is not being disloyal to be able to appreciate these things. Your loved one is gone but they would want you to look for some way of feeling better. By doing these small things regularly you can ease yourself into accepting what is.

To what do I attribute my successful experience in dealing with my father's death? I was able to access a different perspective and then see he was a victim as well as his father and grandfather. It was passed down through the generations to have uncontrollable anger. My father decided it would end with him and he was ultimately successful. He loved me (and my siblings) more than life itself and created the ability for all to move forward in life. We come here to learn and grow and his life was successful, as has mine been. I love my father as never before because of who he became.

My *Unwavering Strength* is that I persisted until I was able to find these old stories and work on them until they were deactivated; I looked for unresolved issues and changed my perspective.

About the Author

Jeanne Henning is a Best Selling Author with her book "If I Loved You, What Would I Tell You?" She has also written "Uplifting Messages" which are teachings accompanied by beautiful pictures she has taken in her extensive traveling around the world. Jeanne has studied the Masters to become an expert in Spirituality and living life. She has been a Registered Nurse for many years. www.JeanneHenning.com.

Escape from Behind the Iron Curtain

Silke Nied

"You are never strong enough that you don't need help."
—César Chávez

I was born long after the wall known as the Iron Curtain was built, splitting Germany into East and West. As an East German, I lived under an oppressive communist regime. I grew up thinking I'd never be free to speak my mind or travel. We couldn't visit relatives in West Germany because the communist government knew we might defect. Officially, the wall was built to keep "enemies" out, but everyone knew it was to keep East Germans captive. Many people tried to escape. Some were successful, but many were killed in the attempt. Never in my wildest imagination did I think my parents would risk attempting to leave. Why did they want to start a new life at forty? The answer was simple—Freedom.

Our first escape attempt began discreetly. In the summer of 1978, we prepared for our vacation as usual. We traveled along the Danube in Romania until we reached a campground. I'd been asleep for several hours when soft voices woke me. I realized my uncle was there. Eager to see him, I almost jumped out of bed when what I heard froze the blood in my veins. My parents were planning to escape East Germany! I lay still, afraid to breathe.

The next morning, my mother said, "Silke, look who came to visit us." I acted surprised, and even more so when they told me what I already knew.

We observed the river for a few days looking for a spot to swim safely across to what was then Yugoslavia. This was no small feat, but eventually we found what we thought was the perfect place. Later when we decided it was time to go I was so afraid that my uncle gave me medicine to calm me. The dose was too much for my young body. I became so groggy that our plan had to be aborted. The miscalculation had a fortuitous result—that night the moon was full. It would've allowed the border patrol to spot us easily. Sadder but wiser, we headed home to East Germany.

We tried again two days later, but it was impossible to get in the water without being shot at by the shore patrol. We understood we wouldn't escape that year. It was hard living in East Germany after that, having almost tasted freedom.

We continued planning our escape. We trained to swim the Danube's cold three-kilometers. We studied the almanac to plan our vacation by a new moon. Lucky for us, we had our cabin at the lake, which meant we could take our fins and swim for hours without anyone suspecting. When it got cold, we swam in our local public pool.

July 1979

Our time finally arrived. We behaved as normally as possible around friends and family before leaving for our supposed vacation. By the end of summer we'd be free! With hearts pounding, we drove away.

My uncle met us in Orsova, and we camped close to the Danube. Some fellow campers joined us, and mentioned the border patrol shot at people and left them in the water to break for shore—if they managed to survive the bullets! I was scared to death.

On the night of July 19th, my uncle drove us to a bay. He continued on to a hotel where his room faced the bay, an important detail since he'd signal us when it was safe to start. We sat for hours waiting for darkness and our signal which would be Uncle Dietmar standing on the balcony with his arms outstretched.

I was delegated the task of crawling up the bank to check for his signal. This was a huge responsibility for a fourteen-year-old. It was life or death for my family, and the gravity of it was palpable. My guardian angel led me to the correct window.

Crawling back to my parents, I told them we could leave. Even in July, the Danube is frigid, so my mother rubbed thick skin cream on everyone's arms to shield us from the cold. Entering the water, we set out for freedom. I had no fear; in fact, I had no feelings at all. I felt like we were in a trance, running on pure adrenaline. We swam smoothly, making few waves, my mother to my left and my father to my right. It was quiet, eerie, and unreal.

We had fresh clothing tied to our backs with important documents wrapped in plastic. As we swam, our clothing got heavier and heavier. This wasn't our only problem. At the halfway point, a Romanian patrol boat appeared with its searchlight probing. Reflexively, I whispered, "Dive!" When we surfaced, the searchlight came around again, so we dove a second time. The patrol boat moved on. We were too close for its beam to target us.

Just when we thought we were home free, we spotted lights moving in front of us. A ship! Had our timing been different by mere minutes, we would likely have been caught in its propeller. Thanking God, I swam on, praying my legs would hold out. My mother must have noticed my exhaustion, because she dragged me the last few meters to shore.

We made it! We were alive and free! Our newfound freedom didn't last long. A barking border patrol dog and its handler came out of the brush. The guards ordered us in Russian not to move. I can still hear my mother begging them not to shoot us. They bound our hands with heavy cords, then pushed us through the brush toward the road, to begin walking, soaking wet, to the nearest detention station.

At the station, the guards offered us dry clothes, hot tea, and aspirin. Pretty soon, we'd warmed up enough for the captain to interrogate us. He kept us up all night with questions and sent some officers to the river to check for accomplices. My uncle was questioned regarding his identity, but no one asked my mother her maiden name, a connection that linked them.

The next day we went to the city station for further questioning. Another station. More questions. They were going to separate us. Our captors thought we were strangers until after almost a day's worth of discussion, they understood we were a family. Finally, they placed us in one cell. At least we were together.

The police chief decided my mother and I should stay at a hotel. We were assigned a third floor room because the chief said if we were crazy enough to swim the Danube, we were crazy enough to jump out the first floor window.

A movie theater across the way helped us tell time. We figured the evening show started at 8 pm. Every now and then, the police chief brought my father to see us and to shave and shower. Sometimes the chief even took my mother and me to lunch or for a walk. No one seemed to know what to do with us, but I strongly believe the police chief's getting to know us worked in our favor.

One day a man dressed in a black suit came to our room. He took us to the police station to meet my father and board a bus to Belgrade, Yugoslavia's capital. My mother and I thought it was a set-up to make us to do something stupid and get sent back to East Germany. With great reluctance, we went with the man in black.

We met my father at the station, and the chief took us on the bus to Belgrade. Aboard the tacky, overheated bus, we sat in uncomfortable seats for a miserable twelve-hour ride with dozens of stops. My mother noticed the gun in the chief's pants, but she never mentioned it because she knew I'd be terrified.

We finally reached Belgrade. The chief took us to a hotel for refugees. Expenses were paid by the country granting asylum, West Germany. We said good-bye to the chief, who was partly responsible for guiding us to freedom. I will never forget him.

We were unsure of what to do next. The attendant told us someone from the United Nations would contact us. About an hour later, a young, blonde, handsome man came to our door. The UN, he said, was handling our case now. He gave us directions to the West German Embassy and money for food. That night, my parents were so excited, they could hardly sleep.

When we reached the embassies our hearts raced when we spotted an East German guard. We walked boldly past him to the West German embassy next door. Of course, the guard couldn't know we'd recently escaped his country. We felt like we had escapee written all over us. We triple-checked our surroundings to be certain we were at the West German embassy. Its flag left little doubt, still, my mother asked the guard if we were in the right place. When he assured her we were, my parents began to cry. We were free!

Inside, one of the embassy staff worked to get us passports. I will never forget her name: Mrs. Pempelforth. She told us we'd be taking the train to Giessen to register at an office of the West Germany government.

We hadn't time to buy food before boarding the train for a twenty-four hour ride. Well into our journey, we reached the Yugoslavian/Austrian border. While we rode, my uncle drove from Romania back to West Germany. With no sign of us, he'd given us up for dead and burnt our fake passports. He later said it felt like he was destroying us as he set fire to them. For two more weeks, he kept watch for us anyway before returning home.

Meanwhile, we continued our journey to Giessen. Upon arrival we discovered we were free to go as long as we returned on Monday. My mother phoned my aunt and told her. My aunt said, "Okay, we'll come visit you tomorrow." Still in a daze, she hadn't comprehended what my mother said. But Uncle Dietmar did. "I'm going up there right now to get them!" he practically leapt into his car with my aunt's husband.

We waited for him in the train station parking lot. Suddenly, we spotted his car tearing around the corner. Jumping from it, he ran to us and hugged and kissed us. "Silke," he said, choked up, "I can't believe you made it."

A huge audience had gathered at our parking lot reunion. I glanced down at my uncle's feet and burst out laughing. He wore only socks. He was so excited he'd forgotten to put his shoes on!

This is my story. I've shared it for the sake of my children in the hope that they'll never take freedom for granted, because where I grew up, it could be taken away in an instant. Today, when I reflect that my children and I live in the freest country in the world, I'm filled with gratitude for my parents who had the courage and unwavering strength to risk their lives and mine for this opportunity.

About the Author

Silke Nied lives in Gig Harbor, Washington. She has two sons, 26 and 18, and a six-year-old grandson. She lived in East Germany until she was 14 and then in West Germany until she turned 27. She and her five-year-old son came to Washington in 1992 after she married a military man. She had planned to stay for two years, yet has remained in the U.S. for 22 years. Her parents still live in Germany and so does Uncle Dietmar. "Never in my dreams would I have imagined living here. It's an awesome feeling to know that you can do anything you put your mind to and are never too old to do it." —Silke

The Blueberry Muffin

Evelyn Roberts Brooks

*"The purpose of life is to live it, to taste experience to the utmost, to
reach out eagerly and without fear for newer and richer experience."*
—Eleanor Roosevelt

The lace-draped dining table displayed homemade cakes, covered
casseroles, and lattice-topped pies. Neighbors and friends from church
paraded in and out, bringing words of comfort . . .and comforting
food. As arriving guests found space for their offerings and then joined others
in the living room, a small hand crept from beneath the table and snatched
a blueberry muffin.

Hiding under the tablecloth, a skinny blonde girl, age nine, bit into the
muffin. A finicky eater, she had a weakness for sweets, but her pleasure was
spoiled by a belief it was sinful to enjoy a treat at such a time.

I was that girl, and I remember that crisp sunny November afternoon
in north Texas as if it was yesterday, although it was over 50 years ago. My
brother had just died, after two years of operations, anxious nursing, and
countless prayers to try to save him from the ravages of a cancerous brain
tumor. He was four years old.

I was no stranger to grief, but it was not a welcome companion.

Four years earlier, my sister who was three had died during an operation
meant to relieve her hydrocephalic condition of spinal fluids in her brain.

During my brother's illness, my youngest sister was born, making seven
children, six girls and one boy, with me in the middle. She had a severe case of
cerebral palsy caused by oxygen deprivation at birth. Her mind never developed although her body did; she died later at age 18.

The year after my brother's death, we received news that the girl who had been my best friend before moving to another state had died of a brain tumor.

People I loved came and went, while I watched helplessly.

I shrank from the pity and curiosity of others. I pretended I was fine. Grief settled around my shoulders like an unwanted cloak as heavy as wet clay. It dried and hardened, trapping me within.

Soon after my brother's funeral, my mother came into our bedroom with a large empty carton and began filling it with toys, books, and gifts given to cheer him during his illness. I heard her whisper, "I can't bear having to do this again!"

My feet were frozen to the floor. I knew I should help her, but I was angry she didn't ask if I wanted any of the toys for myself.

When she left, I snatched a book from the box. It was A Child's Garden of Verses by Robert Louis Stevenson. My brother Philip's name was on the front page. The writing was my own, because I had placed a pencil in his small hand when the book was new and helped him sign his name. Now I carefully erased his name, wrote mine over the remaining traces and hid the book in my dresser. The book was all I had of my brother, and each time the family moved to a new city, I packed the book and took it—took him— along with me. Today, that book is still one of my most treasured belongings.

Events hold different explanations in a young mind which is grasping for understanding. Undisclosed secrets keep a child trapped in the iron grip of feeling unloved and unlovable. The complicated inner workings of a child's mind led me into a lifetime of silence about my younger brother and two younger sisters. I picked up cues from those around me, and never talked about them, or about my feelings. My childhood terrors that I would be the next to die were blanketed by silence.

I sought forgetfulness, unaware that what I needed to discover was the power of self-forgiveness.

Unhealed grief doesn't vanish with time. It goes underground and wreaks its havoc. Although I went through the semblance of falling in love (more than once), and raising my beloved daughter, the long-held belief that I was somehow to blame for what happened to my younger siblings kept me from experiencing genuine love and success.

I tried to slam the door on the past, but I'd be eating a blueberry muffin during a business conference and suddenly have to choke back scalding tears. I'd remember the guilt-ridden episode from my brother's funeral and push it down, refusing to think about it. But in that refusal, I kept myself stuck in endless grief.

That book of poetry I used to read to my brother includes "My Shadow." I recall the opening lines: "I have a little shadow that goes in and out with me, and what can be the use of him is more than I can see."

It took many years for me to see that all the shadows in my life stemmed from my unhealed grief and survivor's guilt. I felt isolated and alone, even though I was adept at smiling and acting as if my life was as good on the inside as it appeared on the outside.

Trying to force forgetfulness was a solution that backfired on me. By dismissing my grief and asserting that everything was okay I stunted my own emotional and spiritual growth. My untrained groping for happiness inadvertently led me into more pain and confusion in codependent relationships. I dismissed my own feelings, and failed to set boundaries, oblivious to the inner core of strength which was waiting for me to acknowledge and activate it.

The heart is resilient. It only fails to heal when we cling to an old story of unbearable sorrow.

Each person arrives with a message of love. Some deliver their message within an hour and then depart, others of us live into another century. Brief or long, our journeys all end in love and joy. While we are here, it's up to us to make our life worthwhile. Fun. Love. Creativity. That's what we came for.

I wanted my freedom from grief and I was determined to get it. I began taking a journey of the heart I'd been avoiding, and the first step was to recognize there's always a payoff in everything we do. As a child, hiding my pain helped me feel safer, but that coping tool became chains.

I was unaware that I had the alchemist's power to transform sad memories from a leaden weight into pure gold.

Grief is not meant to be a parking space—it's a springboard. Living small didn't bring them back. But living big could honor them, and help others.

Searching for answers led me to books about life after life, and how to enjoy a purpose-driven life. Meditation showed me how to relax and allow shimmering light to fill every cell and cleanse away the pain.

Living in the past put the brake on my life mission of helping others to be joyful. I stopped defining myself by my losses and realized how much I could help others because of the experiences I'd survived. I learned to thrive.

I began gifting myself with adventures into the past, where I cast a fond look at my family and envisioned us healing with love. I surrounded myself with furniture that had belonged to my parents and with photos and mementos that remind me of my family. I replaced self-blame with kindness and gentleness towards myself, freeing myself from old ideas that kept me from living a joyful life.

I found comfort in sponsoring a poor child through a charitable organization, so that I can offer hope for her better life in memory of my long-lost siblings.

I integrated my wounded little girl by recognizing what she experienced and loving her. I opened my heart wide, and then wider still. The little shadows of my younger self, of my three younger siblings, are all with me, but now they are laughing, happy, and sharing my journey.

Stuck in long-standing grief, I felt weak, and unworthy of shining in life. Fully integrated with my history, I became strong, invincible, and ready to beam out a message of hope for others. That heavy clay cloak cracked and fell away, revealing the folded wings that had been there all along.

Several years ago, the year after I was widowed, I lost nine friends in one year to cancer, including my best friend of 30 years. The next year, two of my beloved dogs died. I had the choice of buckling under, or seeing that our loved ones are never lost to us. They are simply gone from sight.

My experiences have taught me that I have a choice about my attitude, and I choose happiness each day. By embracing all aspects of my journey, including the parts I had labeled painful and sad, I learned how to tap into the bottomless well of unwavering strength that we all have access to.

Life is somewhat like a blueberry muffin. We can focus on the squished berries, the lopsided muffin top, and the crumbs—or we can savor the overall sweetness and delight.

Today I celebrate life and I can even do it by happily eating a blueberry muffin and reading a childhood book of poetry. Life is a banquet—go out and taste the love and joy it offers!

About the Author

Evelyn Roberts Brooks is a bestselling author (Forget Your Troubles, You Were Born to Triumph and ten other books), success coach, speaker, and founder of Born to Triumph®. Evelyn's books, programs, and in-depth coaching show you how to reduce your stress, feel happier, and lead a more empowering and joyful life. Claim your bonus gift at www.evelynbrooks.com

Finding Real Perfection

How My Neurosis Led Me to Discover My True Nature

Daniel Parmeggiani

"Perfectionism is a self destructive and addictive belief system that fuels this primary thought: If I look perfect, and do everything perfectly, I can avoid or minimize the painful feelings of shame, judgment, and blame."
—Brené Brown

They say it is darkest before the dawn. I don't know if that's a factual statement or just an illusion created by tired, sleepy morning eyes, but this cliché accurately describes my personal spiritual path. Just when my life seemed completely doomed, a miracle happened. I awakened to my absolute innocence, and in that innocence, I found the key to self-forgiveness, non-judgment, and self-love.

A series of traumatic events during my childhood created deep guilt, self-doubt, a crippling social phobia, and a growing sense that there was something terribly wrong with me. For years I endured constant taunting and bullying in school and kept it all to myself, ashamed of what I had become.

Then the Obsessive Compulsive Disorder (OCD) kicked in.

In an attempt to cope, my mind subconsciously came up with two twisted beliefs that would lead me down a hopeless path of self-destruction. The first belief was that I had to be perfect. The second was that it was always my fault when I wasn't perfect. My young mind had concluded that per-

73

fection was always required and that there was never a valid excuse to be anything but flawless. It was an ideal recipe for a life of constant failure, paralyzing fear, and inescapable guilt.

Before I knew it, OCD had seized complete control over my mind. Whether I was playing sports, organizing my closet, or brushing my teeth, the frightful demand for perfection was always present, turning every moment of my life into a tense and anxious inner battle. Everyday tasks like writing became painstakingly tortuous. My penmanship demanded perfection, and the natural flow of my hand was inhibited by the need to consciously control the shape of every letter of every word. The result was chicken scratching that would make a doctor proud.

I was stuck in a perpetual struggle to reach the unreachable, and failure was not an option! Yet I did fail every time, and every time, the whip of my own guilt and condemnation would strike with all its might and force me to stand up and try again. I was supposed to be perfect, and it was always my fault when I wasn't. Maybe I was completely nuts after all.

When I was 15, a psychologist tried to explain my disorder to me. This was the first time I had ever heard about perfectionism or obsessive-compulsive disorder, but the things he said rang true. I felt like somebody finally understood me. This breathed new life into me and renewed my sense of hope. However, there was a problem: He understood me, but I did not understand him.

My vision of the world was so ingrained in my personality that I was not willing to let it go—not unless I was perfectly convinced that it was perfectly safe to do so. Therefore, for the next two years, I obsessed day and night over everything that was discussed in therapy. I analyzed myself continuously, trying to untangle the spaghetti code inside my mind. I felt that I had to understand it all perfectly, or else I would be stuck forever. I required perfect arguments, perfect certainty, and perfect proof! Otherwise, I would not be capable of accepting any sort of change.

My perfectionism was like a living entity that I could not defeat. This self-created monster had a fool-proof defense system because I would never be able to come up with a perfect case to overthrow it. I began to truly believe that there was no way out for me. Little did I know that something truly amazing was about to happen.

My quest for the perfect answers would definitely have led me to a mental institution had it not been for a miraculous turn of events. When I was 17, on one especially dark day, I broke down. I sensed that there was no hope in what I was doing, and I felt completely lost. The familiar gut-wrenching guilt tried to spur me back into the battle. But this time, I did not respond. My will was broken, and I finally gave up.

For several hours, I sat quietly in a daze. Then suddenly, out of sheer desperation, I began to pray, "God, tell me what I must do to find my way out of this hell."

At first it was a sobbing whisper, but then my pleading gradually gained strength. I would do anything, anything! Please just tell me what I need to do!

Next came anger, a deep red, boiling anger. My words became furious demands for answers. I screamed at the top of my lungs, rebelling against my rotten life, my stupid parents, my unfair world, and my uncaring God. It's not my fault! It's not my fault! IT IS NOT MY F'ING FAULT!

I rebelled against my guilt.

To this day, I do not know how or why it happened. Maybe a higher energy or consciousness intervened, or maybe it was just me finally reaching absolute rock bottom. All I know is the relief I felt was so great that I could not stop laughing and crying.

This outpouring of bottled up emotion went on for at least an hour, after which a state of serenity and lightness unlike any I'd ever felt took over my whole being. Suddenly disconnected from the terrible demands of my inner judge, I felt great joy just lying there in my room staring at the ceiling. I stayed there, feeling no need to get up to accomplish or fix anything. I did not experience my usual asthma attacks when I thought I was wasting time, and I was not concerned about what was imperfect in my life.

With surprising ease, I realized that I had been right to forgive myself, and I knew exactly why.

From my new perspective, I could see that it wasn't my fault that I was stuck in my misery. I understood that all I ever wanted was to get better—to feel better. I could see that happiness was my only goal and that only ignorance was keeping me from reaching that goal. Had I known with certainty what I needed to do to find lasting relief, I would already be doing it, regardless of the sacrifices involved. If ending my suffering required eating broken glass, I would have smashed a window, eaten my fill, and asked for seconds.

For the next few days, I couldn't help but obsess about what had happened. Then a strange but satisfying thought surfaced in my mind:

I am always doing the best I can to get closer to happiness.

As it turned out, that simple phrase gave me the unwavering strength to pull myself out of my misery and embark on an incredible journey of spiritual self-discovery. In time, I realized that we all share the same ultimate goal, the same single underlying motivation for everything we do. This goal guarantees that we are incapable of being anything but innocent.

Awareness of my true, innocent nature released me from my own self-torture and allowed me to see others through the eyes of non-judgment, compassion, and unconditional love.

As my perception shifted from the darkest black of night to the bright light of dawn, the door to true, lasting inner peace opened before me. Life forced me to know myself at the deepest level, and I found that we do not need to strive for perfection. We are already perfect just the way we are.

About the Author

Daniel Parmigianni was born in Caracas, Venezuela, and moved to the U.S when he was 12. Growing up in a household traumatized by the violent death of his older brother and caught between two radically different parental worldviews, young Daniel often felt guilty, isolated, and depressed. Finally at age 17, he experienced a profoundly cathartic vision of self-forgiveness and self-love. Feeling it was his responsibility to present this important spiritual message to the world, Daniel wrote his first book, The Magnificent Truths of Our Existence. Daniel spent ten years working successfully in the field of computer science. He then became a day-trader in the stock market, which he continues to this day. He currently lives in Pompano Beach, Florida with his wife Susan and their dog Chewy. www.MagnificentTruths.com

The Divorce That Enlightened My Life

Anya Sophia Mann

"This too shall pass..."
—Sufi proverb

I am dying inside with my two children in the back seat on December 1, 1987 mid afternoon. Exactly 18 years earlier I walked down the elegant aisle of a New England church to vow, "I do." It was my wedding day. Now, today, the situation that is unfolding will impact like the reverberation from the shock waves of a sonic boom. This is the day my heart cracks wide open causing a bleed that will last for years.

Parking in my usual spot at work to collect my paycheck, a man that I did not recognize approaches my car, calls my name and asks if that is me. Smiling I say yes, keenly aware of my pre-teen daughter and son, silent, behind me. With his hand firmly extended he reaches into my open car window. I have no choice but to take from his hand the papers that now block my view. His deep voice, raspy and strong, shivers down my spine as I hear his ice cold words pierce my interior echoing loudly, "Mam, you have just been served divorce papers."

Months earlier at the breakfast table, I felt deeply sad, yet at peace when we told the children of our mutual decision that we thought it was best to divorce. The decision brought relief from the haunting, soul-stealing pain of our escalating 'irreconcilable differences.' My relief, short lived, is soon consumed by the searing heartache that becomes my new bed partner. Days and nights are taken hostage by schizophrenic-like emotions, drowning my innate happiness. This unexpected head-on emotional collision to my heart, and the ensuing debilitating paralysis, sharply contrasts my feelings of that earlier Sunday morning.

Under the guise of the legal protection of our lawyers we stand before the Judge. In a firm direct voice so nothing can be misunderstood by anyone the Judge, motionless, declares, "this marriage is dead. This divorce is final." He then leans forward drawing us all closer as if in collusion and says without compassion, "It is now official. Act as if this marriage had never happened."

Screeching to a halt inside, my guts scream righteously to any God that will hear me, "my children, what about my children? Are they now declared dead too?"

At thirty-nine, legally single, still stunned and shocked in the grip of terror, I walk aged and lifeless down the aisle of the courtroom. Naked, raw in vulnerability, I move past the view of my teenage sweetheart. The handsome man of my childhood dreams who became my husband and the father of my children. He looks at me with glistening tears of sadness in his eyes and, stopping me, he quietly says, "You were a wonderful mother." And on that note, with those exact words, I had no idea that that too was about to change.

Descending the grey steps outside the courtroom thoughts shoot into my mind like bullets, "Oh my God! I have no lifeline! I have no one to turn to! No one to call when the car breaks down. No one to talk to in the middle of the night. No one to reassure me at times like right now, this very instant."

Panicking, I urgently want to run back, breathless with fear and terror pleading, "I'm scared to death! Help me!" The first smack of reality hits hard and fast. A death certificate in the form of a divorce, now in hand from an 18-year marriage to a man I met and fell in love with when I was 17.

The months that follow would make or break me. A finely furnished home reduced to a modest apartment. All the furniture was in storage, until a phone call announcing that everything has gone up in smoke in a fire. My heart sinks as I realize the family photos are now gone too. A week later, I am frightened in the pitch dark of night, waiting to be rescued in my broken down car. "Unrepairable" the body shop tells my blank eyes.

This begins the cascade of amputations that cut me off from the world I used to know. What is happening to me? How am I going to cope? That question had all the answers in it. I cope by paying attention to how I am coping and through that see the buried qualities in me that are coming alive.

Bleeding my feelings to a friend she recommends her therapist. The next day we begin the arduous work of peeling layers that will eventually liberate my soul. I begin with telling her that all of my married life has exploded. I learned a single question that reveals the empowering qualities I need to create a new life. I ask everyday "Where am I showing strength today?" The answers are in noticing the little ways I am creating movement in my shattered life. Some days it is the basics of getting up and showering. Other days it is the big ones like being at the mall and weeping while walking without my children's hands in mine, or eating my dinner without crying because I have (yet again) shopped for and cooked a meal for four, in denial that there is only me now.

I have an unwavering faith that all is happening for a higher purpose beyond anything I could ever possibly reason. It is the only thing that makes sense in my life. I surrender all pain to that knowing. Like the ripping sheer agony of living without my children. While visiting their Dad 3,000 miles away they fall in love with gorgeous California. Calling me they ask excitedly, "Can we live here Mom?" "Yes, of course!" An innocent decision that nearly kills my soul. The trajectory of my family life changes forever. Blinded and broken, I must now carve a new life without any tools or a guide. I have to. Or die.

Sharing feelings of lack of love and not being 'seen' in my marriage, I get the biggest wake up call of my life, shifting my perception about everything forever. My therapist says to me in the perfect moment, "You can't make a blind man see!" Dear God I get it! I have been trying to get people to 'see me' when for their own unique reasons, they can't. It is my job to see me, not theirs. A new 'me' was born in that moment. The profound understanding and calming clarity that came with those words evoked a precise knowing that lit up as pure truth in my heart and soul. A whole new world was about to be birthed, by a virgin me.

No more jagged edges. They were smoothed out by rubbing up against heaping mounds of struggle, turmoil and chaos. All put in my path by life, to stretch and grow me out of denial and low self-esteem. It is so different for me now as I reap the wisdom bravely earned that oozed from healed wounds. I know what happened with me is not who I am. My saving grace was finding a connection to my true, real, authentic self. Safely emerged from behind the protection of blinders, I can see me now. I came to realize that an unwavering strength had been my constant companion, like a guiding angel, supporting me and growing me, at the same time. A spiritual gravitation from my soul that I had to integrate fully in order to live more connected in myself. The one who was there all along, throughout the riveting, revealing, enlightening journey of divorce.

Today, finally unafraid, my heart wide open and my mind free, I am sitting in my home, across from a crackling fire. It is nearly dawn in the desert of Arizona where I live. My daughter and her family also reside nearby. My senses are enriched by the fresh aroma of a cup of coffee at my side. I am caressed by gentle, melodic piano music, thoughtfully chosen to grace the environment for the task at hand. I share with you the scene I am breathing in, for a reason. Sitting here with fingers dancing on my keyboard, I am writing with inner clarity, what you are reading right now. It is December 25, 2013 Christmas Day. It feels like a full circle moment in many ways. My adult children are in California with their Father, stepmother, stepbrother and sister. My beautiful young grandchildren are with them. This holiday, I am embraced in the warmth of the reality that I can now happily be with myself. Forgiven, as evidenced by the absence of volatile waves of crushing abandonment. A mighty transition from the past losses that crushed me unrecognizably. I am here with myself. In peace. What matters most to me now, is the ability to love unconditionally, and "I do!"

About the Author

Anya Sophia Mann, a Visionary Intuitive Consultant, provides coaching and mentoring for transformational personal and professional growth. She has excelled in the field of human development for over 25 years through workshops, seminars, retreats, and her private consultancy. She loves her roles as a public speaker, writer, published author, Founder and Editor of LifeCoachingMagazine.NET, Producer and Host of 'Quantum Alchemy Radio' featuring, among others, 'Unwavering Strength' radio show. She is author of "Born Connected: Life In The World Of A Visionary Intuitive." Visit AnyaSophiaMann.com.

Beyond the Ordinary

The Unwavering Power of Love

John Burgos

"In dying comes the opportunity for resurrection and for building new dreams. The story can be honored, the memories can be cherished and we can marvel as a new foundation is poured. Our soul knows the path. Remember to tap into the unwavering strength that is innate within and trust that it will lead to your divine destination."
—John Burgos

W hy is it that we need to experience emotional turmoil? The truth is that heart-wrenching situations can be catalysts, designed precisely, to lead us onto the next level of the journey to our destinies. Arduous paths become easier to navigate when we become aware of our innate gifts and powerful capacities. I have come to befriend the opportunities leading me to my soul's calling that have come disguised as pain and challenges.

Grief is a gift with a purpose. When our hearts are broken we experience unexpected threads in our life's journey to navigate. And although we may suffer a symbolic or a literal death to mourn, we are also presented with a golden opportunity, divinely orchestrated by the Universe, to lead us in a new direction. In hindsight, grief has been a catalyst that helped me to realize that I had become a stranger to my greatest talents, my intuition and empathy. I found that through the power of my sixth sense and the unwavering strength that it incites, I could connect to the wisdom in my heart and make the empowered choices that fill my soul with joy and purpose.

I never quite fit into a box. I remember being able to walk into a room and know what others were thinking and feeling. It was this innate ability that helped me to develop my chameleon-like ability to inconspicuously fit in, help to keep the peace and not create any ripples so that I would be accepted. The fewer waves I made the safer I felt. I understand now that I am, and have always been, an empathic intuitive.

I grew up in a home with parents who had a very loving relationship as long as dad was sober. When he drank, which was every evening, my senses went on high alert. By the age of four, I chose to make it my job to stay awake all night so that I could be on guard and ready to react to any hint that another altercation was brewing. Our home was a volatile war zone and this abusive environment was evidenced in the hidden bruises my mother had to hide and the emotional roller coaster we all endured. Although my brother and I were never physically harmed, the trauma that the emotional scars left behind affected us profoundly. My parent's fights were hideous, Mom screamed obscenities at dad and he frequently would pull a kitchen knife threatening to kill her. Adding to the injury was the aloof response of our family and friends who were aware of the abuse yet chose to do nothing. What would you do if you learned that your four-year-old child had stepped in between a knife wielding, alcohol-induced maniac and an enraged woman whose pride trumped her survival instincts in his effort to stop the violence?

If you understand that the abuse was normal to our friends and family, it helps. Ignorance was safer than confrontation. However, I knew there was a cure for any conflict, love. I don't remember when I gave up believing that love was the answer, but when I did, the world as I understood it, the mystical realm of infinite possibilities, the communication with my guides, and of feeling benevolently protected, appeared to have died with it.

I was seventeen years old and remember the dream as if it were yesterday. I felt as if was spinning in a whirlwind of energy but it was not the daunting, abysmal falling sensation that I recalled from my nightmares as a child. I was traveling through a gateway with visions of orange and bright white lights consuming my field of sight. I had the sensation of flying from one world to the next. I transported in and out of the amazing, blinding light, with its beautiful, luminous glow, I felt a sudden surge of terror slither to the core of my being. My parents died!

Jarred from my sleep, I sprinted to the other side of the house and pounded on my parent's bedroom door. A couple of seconds felt like an eternity until my parents finally responded to my desperate knocks. When I squeezed out the words, and heard their response, I was succumbed by tears of relief. Their voices were all I needed to hear. My parents were alive, yet the dream felt so real.

This dream was profound in that it stirred within me a capacity to grieve that I did not know I was capable of. I had never contemplated the certainty that one day my parents would die. But I also KNEW someone had died!

The next day my dream proved to be a forewarning. While I was at soccer practice, mom received a distressing long distance call. Her father had passed away during the evening.

It all made sense. It wasn't a dream. I knew it was a connection that I physically experienced in this dimension to that which had yet to occur. I kept what I understood to myself. My parents never talked about or mentioned my previous night's vision and I didn't feel the need to have my insights validated by them at the time. Mom and dad were consumed with grief and needed their space to mourn.

This esoteric revelation could have led me to explore my capacity to tap into a higher awareness and use it as a guidepost, but instead I dismissed its power as something ordinary. However, I intuitively started to see a pattern was taking form. Memories ignited into my awareness reminding me that the intuitive hits and metaphysical experiences that I encountered as a child were still alive.

I also had a perplexing dream of my uncle, Oscar, visiting me to tell me goodbye. The next morning we received the news that he had passed away from a stroke the night before. I mentioned the dream to my parents, who again, in their state of mourning, dismissed my insight as an ordinary occurrence.

As penetrating as these dreams and visions were, they were only a glimpse into the information that I would receive as I continued to live my ordinary existence. I did my best to carve out a small niche in which I could finally feel safe. Looking back, it became obvious that I was being given the pieces to a roadmap to find where I belonged, but the feelings of home and community eluded me. The problem was that I continued looking for this haven through the lens of external influences. I wanted a successful career, a happy marriage and my own children to raise the right way.

In July of 1990, a week before I was to be married, my fiancé blindsided me with her doubts about the impending ceremony. My reaction was that if Mindy wasn't ready, then we should call off the ceremony. I honored her emotions, and I refused to try to talk her into marrying me. Mindy dismissed her fear blaming it on the normal pre-wedding jitters and convinced me that I was the man she wanted to be with for the rest of her life.

A week later we walked down the aisle. The ceremony was beautiful. The pastor delivered a heart inspired sermon. Our guests beamed with approval and Mindy was glowing. After the "I do's" the reggae band started the party and the dance floor quickly filled up. That's when it hit me! An overwhelmingly dizzying feeling that forced me to leave the reception and sequester myself into a back room.

I closed my eyes and sat in silence. Suddenly I was overcome with a sensation of celestial love and heard a gentle whisper saying " You will be married eighteen years."

Part of me knew that this prophecy would come true but I didn't run from what I knew was my destiny. I knew to trust that familiar, loving voice that felt like the home I had always longed for. The fate of our marriage was predetermined but I trusted that my love for my wife was real and that we had a course that we were destined to chart together.

Our marriage did end after eighteen years. We did have love, adventures, challenges, and two beautiful daughters. In many ways our relationship was successful, and when it all came tumbling down, where the grief ultimately led me was to a beautiful gift of awakening.

Our journey was divinely orchestrated to put me onto the fast track to a profound transformation. I rewired my limiting beliefs, reformatted my cellular memories and owned the undeniable fact that my empathetic abilities and sensitivity were a gift, not a sign of weakness.

Through the divorce and the omens that appeared as precursors to our separation, I was able to gain back pieces of my soul which lay dormant. I was learning to have impeccable trust in my intuition and myself. With that trust my soul could begin to heal.

As I resurrected my instinctive gifts, I began to have constructive, fateful, premonitions. I dreamed of leaving old limiting patterns behind, and I had visions of walking though celestial gardens to meet beings from other dimensions who had lessons to teach me. I experienced lucid dreams of flying to majestic mountaintops where instructions leading to my spiritual and psychological evolvement awaited me. They were magical experiences. I felt truly empowered.

I also accessed, what I would later discover to be, warning dreams about the state of my marriage. These dreams were revealing the truth and were hitting me in my blind spots, relentlessly showing me what to heal.

Mindy fulfilled her role as my soulmate by acting as a mirror that I had avoided looking into. She embodied my father's aloofness repeating my parents' patterns. She betrayed my trust, and placed her needs over mine. I finally understood that she played an integral role by reflecting back to me that which I was refusing to see in myself. Why was I not showing up for myself? Why was I betraying myself? When did I stop trusting myself?

Answering the question to these epiphanies was the key that set me free. I remembered with absolute certainty the answer I had as a child, that love IS the answer. I saw past the illusion of the capacity of anybody, including my parents or my ex-wife as being the enemy. I saw past the veils and recognized these souls for the beautiful beings and master teachers that they are. They agreed to show up and help me ignite my purpose. They helped me rediscover that which had never left me, the power that comes from authentically and unabashedly loving myself.

For me empowerment required a profound shamanic journey into forgiveness, which necessitated a commitment to release fear, uncertainty and doubt. Forgiveness of my so-called perpetrators was a beginning, but the cleansing came when I looked in the mirror. From this new perspective I was provided the means to not only serve myself, but also to serve and love others with the enormous capacity I once knew was possible as a child.

Loss can feel as if something within the very essence of your being has vanished forever. Yet all suffering has purpose. At the end of each chapter of our lives comes the promise of a new beginning, a new chapter waiting to unravel with each and every facet of the voyage directed by our heart. Our soul is driven to lead us into experiences that explore and support the unfolding of our destiny. No one can walk the mystery of this realm for us; for this is our own unique shamanic adventure. We are the only ones who can fully comprehend the enormity of the mysterious messages we receive. What we do with this understanding becomes the pivot point for our experience of the transformation waiting to emerge

My pinnacle life events had golden threads that tied them to one another. From the happiest of the circumstance to the darkest, each served a purpose. What I have come to realize is that the Universe is loving and patient and will make sure that we get the message one way or another. Listening and taking action requires the unwavering strength we already possess. Trusting that we posses it is the key. There are no right or wrongs. There are just different choices to make that are designed to always lead us back to love.

About the Author

Inspired by the profound transformational work that resurrected his intuitive abilities, John Burgos decided to leave his successful career in corporate America behind. He trusted his intuition, and he emerged as a gifted and sought-after expert in the personal development industry. Realizing how effectively his work had impacted his clients' lives, John discovered it was his passion and purpose to deliver this new vocabulary and unconventional, multi-dimensional knowledge on a global scale. To achieve that vision he created the transformational series Beyond the Ordinary. This show impacts the lives of tens of thousands of people around the globe and delivers the next generation of thought-provoking inspirational experts to help participants reawaken to life, love and passion. Learn more about John and his international transformational series: www.beyondtheordinaryshow.com

Sex, Drugs, and Death

An Unlikely Spiritual Path

Lisa Clare Barnett

"Yes, I have doubted. I have wandered off the path. I have been lost. But I always returned. It is beyond the logic I seek. It is intuitive—an intrinsic, built-in sense of direction. I seem to find my way home. My faith has wavered but has saved me."
—Helen Hayes

Oh my God, what have I done? I'm trapped. I'm stuck here, again, in this little body with no way out! A flesh and blood person? Really? What was I thinking? No way to communicate. These big people don't understand my baby words. Mommy, I want to go home. I want to go back. I don't know what I was thinking. Haven't I learned all my lessons? Why am I being punished?

These are the memories of a three year old, but they aren't my earliest memories.

I have memories from before I was born into this body. I remember expansiveness, oneness, and all things connected. I remember having form, although not solid. I was pure energy. Connected to everything. No separation. I was fully aware of other light beings' thoughts or feelings. It was a realm without mystery. Everything was clear.

What a shock for a toddler to have an expansive memory, only to be trapped on earth with ineffective communication skills. Fortunately for my family, those memories faded until I was a teenager when my expansive awareness was ignited by the sudden death of one of my best friends.

I was turning thirteen that summer and feeling nervous about starting a new middle school in the fall. One day I was talking to my best friend Marsha on the phone, and the next day she was diagnosed with a brain tumor. She was one of my friends that I considered a soul sister. The other was Shuby. She and I had been soul sisters since we were five years old. We really didn't need anyone else in our tiny sisterhood of two, until we met Marsha. She was sweet and funny, a tiny girl with long, thick black hair. She wore bangs that were too straight accentuating a nose that was still a bit too big for her face. The three of us spent all of our school lunch breaks together. We would often go to Marsha's house to watch *Dark Shadows*, a fabulously funny, yet serious soap opera about a vampire. We lived for that show!

Not long after I moved to California with my family, I got 'the call' from Shuby. She told me that Marsha had undergone brain surgery and was in a coma. Marsha had been having severe headaches and that the doctors had found a tumor. This was devastating news, and to make it more difficult to process, there was no one home to share my pain. I felt so alone, scared, and powerless to help my young soul sister. I had to go to my babysitting job broken hearted. That whole evening I sat alone while the baby slept, crying and praying that Marsha would be ok. I promised God that if he let Marsha live, I would be a good girl and do anything he wanted. I prayed, pleaded, and cried to no avail. A short time later, my dear, sweet Marsha crossed over.

Deep down inside my heart, I knew that no one ever died, that souls go on forever. I intuitively knew that Marsha was fine but I was angry! How unfair! How could God do that to a sweet and innocent child? That anger stayed with me, though it was buried in the darkest corners of my being; that was until my next immense heartbreak.

It was October of 1977; seven years since Marsha died. I was home from college for the weekend. I'd gone out with friends that Saturday night, and when I returned around midnight I noticed that my parents were still up. When I went in to say goodnight they looked at me with heartbreak in their eyes and proceeded to tell me the crushing news. Shuby had been killed in a car accident that evening. She was on the way to a wedding with her boyfriend, when a police car attempted to pull them over. Shuby's boyfriend trying to out run the police lost control of the car. Shuby flew out of the door and had broken her neck upon impact and died.

I couldn't believe my ears. In a short span of time, I lost both Marsha and Shuby. That was too cruel of a realization for a twenty-year-old to endure. I cried deep uncontrollable sobs at the news, and I waited for her soul to come say goodbye before she went into the light. When she didn't come, or at least I couldn't feel her presence; I cried, feeling totally alone. My anger at God returned with vengeance.

The loss of both of my soul sisters was more than my psyche could handle. Over the next few months, I went into a deep depression as I searched for the answer to why I was still alive and they weren't. What kind of God does this? Reading books only triggered the three year old's deep knowing, but that knowing did not offer needed answers. Shuby, a young girl heading off to law school was so bright and beautiful; she seemed to glow with a special light.

Now, she was gone and with her, my faith and trust in a higher power. I knew her soul went on for eternity. I guessed that she must have had some soul contract to leave this life, but I didn't care. I was MAD!!!

At that moment, I consciously decided to take my entire spiritual knowing –all those years of being a student of spirituality—and shove it, literally and energetically, into a shoebox on an imaginary closet shelf out of my sight and life. I saw it all in my mind's eye, clear as day. I slammed that spiritual door closed. I decided what's the use of spiritual knowing if I could not use it to help Marsha or Shuby. My new intentions were to live fully in the physical world, and partake of all of its pleasures: money, fun, tasty food, drink, wonderful sex, and the beauty of nature.

After Shuby left me, nothing seemed right. I was wracked with guilt that I wasn't there to save her. I didn't have much to live for with both my soul sisters gone. After the pain and trauma of that year, I focused on finishing school, beginning my photography career, and making the money I'd promised myself. Though, I had condemned God to a shoebox, believing he/she didn't care; now I know Source was always there.

The summer before Shuby died I'd worked in the Grand Canyon. It was a beautiful place to spend a summer, and I learned to bartend. That skill came in very handy in San Francisco, when I quickly got a job as a cocktail waitress and bartender, helping me pay for photography school.

I lived and worked in a trendy, upscale neighborhood with lots of places for people to drink, party, dance, meet singles, and generally have a wild time. It was the '80s, the time of Michael Jackson, Madonna, leg warmers, and big, off the shoulder sweaters. I drank vodka with grapefruit juice and danced at the discos every night till 2:00 a.m.

I would go to school all day, and on my way home, stop at a local bar for a quick drink, and before I knew it, I had six cocktails lined up in front of me. Everyone knew me. I was a local good time girl.

Often, I would wake up in a stranger's bed, unsure of where I was. It was common for me to take a stranger home at night after downing many cocktails. One of my drinking buddies, Kathleen, was from Ireland. She was a legal assistant by day, and by night, she was my drinking buddy. At the end of every month, we would try to remember the parties we had gone to, the men we had slept with and the different kinds of drugs we'd done.

Whether I was out dancing at a disco on Union Street or drinking in Sausalito, every morning I woke up with a terrible hangover. I'd catch the bus to school; buy a large coffee and off to class. In retrospect, I wonder what my teachers' thought of the cute blonde who was always hung-over. No one seemed to notice or care that I was heading down a destructive path.

I was becoming a good photographer, made new friends from around the world, and got deeper into the bar scene. Some nights after bartending, I would be invited to an after-hours party, where I'd do some cocaine, drink and socialize till dawn.

After graduation, I went job hunting in Chicago. My friends took me out for a goodbye dinner on the way to the airport. I drank way too much, hardly ate, and took a Quaalude with a cocktail. Quaaludes are downers, well, by the time I went to get on the airplane I literally, was falling down drunk. The stewardess took me off the plane, and I passed out in an airport lounge.

When I woke up another airplane was boarding, still so high, I boarded assuming it was a flight to Chicago. When I got to my assigned seat someone was sitting in it, I accused her of taking my seat. She showed me her ticket, and that's when I realized that I was on a plane going to Cleveland, not Chicago. I found a small lounge area where I could sleep it off. By the time I woke up, I had missed another airplane. When I finally got to Chicago, my boyfriend was so mad at me that he no longer wanted anything to do with me. I guess he could see me for the alcoholic I was becoming. No huge loss, I thought to myself. There was always a new job, new boyfriend, and new people to party with.

Early one morning, I was walking home from an all-night binge. I was still wearing my cocktail dress from the night before. I was jittery and exhausted from a whole night of drinking and doing cocaine. I passed a beautiful and sophisticated woman, when a chill ran down my spine. I stopped cold in my tracks. I felt as though I had just seen an angel, in human form. She looked into my soul and I heard, "You are not this! You came to create so much more. Your life has a purpose. Will you throw it away for a drink?"

Thank God, I heard that crystal clear voice ring through my soul. It jolted me from the slumber that my pain had pushed me into. The clear voice of deep truth and reason which that angel spoke on that fateful morning offered me the unwavering strength I needed to let go of my destructive lifestyle. That life covered the depth of my pain and broken heart. It did take years for me to come to grips with the trauma of losing my two dearest friends. I did eventually reconnect to the wisdom and guidance of my soul. Over time, I allowed myself to remember what my three-year-old self knew about the expansiveness and connection of all things. Thank you my unknown beautiful and sophisticated angel that I passed so many years ago. You stopped me in my tracks and saved my life. And, thanks to all the people and angels that kept me safe during those crazy years.

About the Author

Lisa Barnett is an internationally known teacher, consultant and founder of the Akashic Knowing School of Wisdom. Lisa was asked by the Beings of Light from the Akashic Field to bring this ancient wisdom to the world so humanity can be guided by grace. She also teaches students how to clear Karma and release energy that no longer serves them which is often the cause of unnecessary physical, financial and emotional suffering. Lisa specializes in empowering individuals by helping them align with their Soul's Path and incorporate information from their Soul's Library into their life. Through this work Lisa can help you achieve the life your heart and soul desire. www. AkashicKnowing.com

I Will Live Strong– Mark's Story

Mark Lewis

"Courage isn't having the strength to go on - it is going on when you don't have strength."
—Napoleon

This is a story about a man diagnosed with cancer and his fight to beat it every single step of the way.

Mark's journey with Angio Sarcoma began in July of 2011. He had his spleen removed and hoped that the cancer had been beaten.

The prognosis, however, changed in the summer of 2012 when he was told the cancer had spread at a rapid rate and he was given three months to live. All hope was taken away. The doctor said radiation wouldn't help but could alleviate pain. Chemo could extend his life, though only for a couple months.

What better way to have Mark's story told than to share it in his own words. Here are excerpts from Mark's blog. It's a true story of unwavering strength, a story of hope and the story of a man who wasn't going to give up.

I will live strong. My name is Mark. I was diagnosed with Angio Sarcoma. This is my story.

I haven't really taken the time yet to even come to grips with the reality of it all. When the doctor said Angio Sarcoma, I felt relieved because to me it didn't sound so bad. Then the next sentence was, "Please don't Google it because you will be overwhelmed with the information." Umm . . . WOW! Then I had my surgery. Going in to that I felt that if I had my spleen removed there would be "hope." No matter what I read on the Internet or what doctors said, I felt that a miracle could happen. But I was scared. Hundreds of regrets went through my head. I knew in my heart that this wasn't the end. After my surgery the doctor informed us that it would be a long recovery and he would update us on the results of the biopsy from my surgery.

Then I had another doctor's appointment sharing the results of the surgery. The doctor gave us the news that they found and confirmed that I had Angio Sarcoma. I was told that I had to have chemo and it was to start immediately. Even though I was disappointed my thoughts were, "Ok . . . let's do this. I will beat this no matter what it takes."

Chemo was hell . . . I've never felt such pain and sickness. After the follow-up CAT scans it showed that there were no signs of the Angio Sarcoma. I was on cloud nine . . . so much hope that I would beat this. I made it back to work and got back on the fire department and met standards. But after several months I started to feel the pain again, and I knew that something was wrong.

At my next doctor's appointment, my CAT scan showed the cancer had spread at a rapid rate, and I was given months to live. All hope was taken away from me. I looked at Alesha, my wife, and saw how devastated she was and I felt like a failure. I could only think about her and our kids.

I called my uncle Mark with the news. "No, this is not going to happen. We will search for alternative treatment." He said, "I don't care if I have to sell my house, my business, we will find someone that can help you." At that moment I felt hope again. My uncle got in contact with my aunt, and they found a researcher in the States. We had a teleconference, and he explained how there were options. He referred us to treatment in Mexico or Germany. My family and friends came together and did whatever they could to get treatment in Mexico.

The guys from my (fire) hall are doing something incredible for us. They are building my kids a tree fort in the back yard. They will have everything down to their own personal sandbox and deck. I was so touched by the whole thing. This is just want the boys need . . . I always wanted to do that for them. Thank you, guys, for doing this for us. I can't tell you how much I appreciate this amazing gift.

In Mexico, they started me off on mild treatments . . . and I use the word mild loosely. I'm drinking juices that taste like grass and inserting things into places that can stay in Tijuana. They have me on an IV to give me vitamins.

I'm still not sure what tomorrow will look like, but that's when the real treatments start. Aunt Lynda has been a huge support being by my side and asking the questions that should be asked. I told the doctor to give me everything.

My boys start school today. My heart breaks because I can't be with them. Carter I know will be excited, starting a new school and meeting new friends. Tyson, I feel very bad for because he has been in the same school since junior kindergarten and now starting new in grade three. I know how nervous he will be and I wish I could be right beside him this morning encouraging him. I know I will have so many more first school days with my boys. (Mark and Alesha had to sell their house and move in with his aunt and uncle so they would have family close by to help them through this.)

Treatment has gotten tougher and tougher. There have been times when things just seem to never go right, no matter what I do. I feel it's more important than ever to maintain a positive attitude. I feel I will jump back quicker from all of this if I just remain positive. Most days will come out positive for me when I have a positive mindset, but there will be days when nothing seems to work out. I just have to take these days in stride and know that there are better days ahead.

GREAT NEWS!

We were finally seen by the doctor. He explained to us that the CT scan picked up multiple tumors on the bone, and there were no visible tumors on my organs. This was supposed to have taken over my body by now. I was told I was going to be paralyzed within a month and a half and dead within three months. I'm still here, still fighting hard. The doctor explained it appeared that the tumors were healing around themselves.

GREAT NEWS: He isn't offering me palliative care chemo. He wants me to go on a bone hardener so that my bones stay strong and won't break. The doctor explained that my condition is not curable; however, it appears that it hasn't spread throughout my body. This is a huge gain for us.

We had been told there was no hope, but our hope had prevailed. I am so thankful that I have been given the opportunity to fight. I might be in treatment for the rest of my life, but I know I won't stop fighting. I am planning to see our kids' next birthdays and have an 11th anniversary with my wife.

Carpe Diem

Yesterday, while having a therapy treatment, it was discovered that my hernia (from my splenectomy) was possibly interfering with my digestive/

intestinal process. Tests were done, and they showed that I had a bowel obstruction. In addition, there were cancerous lesions located around my body making my pain unbearable. The surgeon wanted to admit me to the hospital to monitor the obstruction and try to clear it. If that didn't work, surgery would be my only other option, but they seemed hesitant about the surgery given my diagnosis of Angio Sarcoma.

Having surgery with severe Angio Sarcoma is definitely not ideal. So for now I fight try to get my pain under control and hope this treatment will work and I will not need the surgery.

Mixed Messages

Last month I was put on a pain pump. I want to wean myself off it. I can interact better with my boys and enjoy the hot tub again. I really just hope to be more mobile. Am I in pain? Yes, of course, but I will be better this way.

I just had an appointment with my oncologist. I was told there is a possible tumor in my abdomen. This news is shocking because during my hospital stay I was told that although I have many lesions in my bones all throughout my body, my organs/soft tissue were cancer free. I now am facing more testing and the possibility of doing chemo.

Miracles happen!

I am sitting in my hospital bed, thankful to be alive. These past few months have been a struggle.

During 2011 when I had my splenectomy to remove my spleen, my diaphragm was nicked. It was apparently very small and a non-issue, given I supposedly only had three months to live. Over these past months the nick had turned into a hole and a hernia had pushed up my colon. The pushed up colon had gotten stuck in the hole in my diaphragm and was strangulated, causing all of my symptoms. Doctors told me unless it was fixed, I would always be feeling sick and most likely unable to have chemo or any other treatments to fight my cancer. In addition, this problem could become life threatening. It was already pushing on my heart and lungs, and it could eventually cause sepsis.

Doctors at the hospital had a lot of differing views. Some thought I had no choice but to attempt the surgery; others thought my body may not be able to survive the surgery and the recovery. After much prayer we were referred to an amazing doctor. During the consultation he told us he had never seen a problem like mine but thought he could help me. I decided to go with the surgery in spite of the potential complications, which were extensive (stomata, cancer spreading, my body being too weak to recover, and damage to my colon). They gave me an almost immediate surgery date of May 7th.

The surgery was a success, and the doctor suspects that I could be involved in some presentations or medical journals. No matter what people say, no one ever knows. Anything can happen if you fight with all you have and put your faith behind what really matters.

Home is wherever I'm with you!

I understand that because of the positive influences in my life, I learned from them and let the negative go. My positive attitude comes from three sources. The first is the commitment to succeed where others will accept failure. The second is the self-confidence that was learned from all the bad times my life. The third is self-respect to overcome the negative to make it a positive learning experience. I hope everyone can learn from my experiences and use it for whatever challenges they might be facing!

Happy trails to yooooou, till we meet again.

After his courageous battle, Mark passed away on February 27, 2014, 2 years and 7 months after his Stage 4 diagnosis.

Mark's beautiful wife Alesha and his two sons, Tyson (8) and Carter (4), gave him the courage and willpower to fight each day with a smile. Mark is the epitome of unwavering strength.

Mark's family would be honored if you would drop by and read his blog for more about his courageous battle: http://livestronger.blog.ca/

My Narrative Healing

Robert McDowell

for Mark Jarman

"Sitting down in a sea of grief to write about grief is a sure way to transform your grief."

It's never good news when the phone rings at 3 a.m.

"It's your sister," my brother's wife said, her voice choking up.

I didn't want to hear more, but I did. After she put her four kids to bed, my sister taped up her garage, wrote a note to our older sister, notes to her kids, settled in behind the wheel of her car, and started the engine. When her son and three daughters woke up expecting cartoons and breakfast, they discovered instead their thirty-six-year-old mother, only hazily visible through a sea of toxic fumes, slumped in her shrouded car.

She was already dead, of course, dead just six weeks after the family had gathered in southern California to bury our mother. Either passage packs a haymaker's punch in a relatively close-knit family, but one death so rapidly following the other took on added weight.

In the keening weekend following our mother's death and leading up to her funeral, as we arrived to celebrate her life and comfort each other, my sister gave no indication that she had been blindsided by more bad news. We only learned after she was gone that she had just lost her job. That was a blow, but none of us could fathom how she felt when her husband, dropping her

97

off at the airport to fly to the funeral, chose that moment to tell her he was in love with another woman and was leaving her.

That internment weekend turned out to be the last time that all of my mother's children were together in this world. All through the weekend, we cried and laughed and told stories; we hugged and took walks and ate meals and just sat quietly together. Yet never in all of that intimate time did my sister once waver in the role she played. She turned out to be a better actress than any of us imagined. She told jokes—more than a few on herself—and laughed more than any of us, but she did not open up her heart.

When news came of my sister's sudden death, how did we feel? Hopeless! Depressed! Forlorn! And yes, bitter, and angry, too. Oh, at times we were furious with her!

But what does it get you to be mad at the dead? It never feels good, it never brings them back, and it even eats away at the images and memories you have of them in your heart and mind. Yes, you tell yourself, that's so true, and minutes later you're cussing them out. If you're lucky, even if you're not particularly awake or making spiritual progress, you get bored hating the dead. You realize it's a negative solution. Isn't it always better to find a more positive alternative? Better yet, wouldn't it be wonderful not to hate the dead at all? Suicides can make that tough to do. Animals don't commit suicide. Trees don't. Even murderous insects refrain from killing themselves. Only we are capable of murdering ourselves.

The poet Robert Penn Warren wrote words to the effect that no matter how you feel about them, when a parent dies, "an umbrella is removed between you and the direful elements." My mother's death felt like that. She was only 67 when she passed, too young, too young. And yet, she'd lived a full and varied life. She'd come to Ellis Island and America from Austria in 1914 when she was less than a year old. In 1918 her parents died, victims of the worldwide influenza epidemic, and three years later, her beloved older sister perished from the same illness. Orphaned, my mother grew up in a Catholic convent and with a couple of not-so-happy foster families.

Even so, family was more important to her than anything else, a fact about her that made sense as we gradually became versed in her difficult childhood marred by the deepest losses. Though I had no name for it as a child, I was aware of the impact those losses had on her. There was something almost imperceptible in her bearing and demeanor that suggested she carried the world's woe on her shoulders, that she was schooled in its shadows and darker truths. It wasn't that she was morose or depressed. She was often quite vivacious. But she possessed gravitas. She was a survivor, a strong woman in an era when women, strong and not so strong, were terribly repressed. A life like hers greatly impacted her children, and when she left us, we were rocked like skiffs in a hurricane. We knew we needed time for processing and grieving, lots of time.

So we were unnerved when so shortly after her death our sister stole the spotlight from her. We were already mad about losing our mom. What right did this troublemaker have to confuse us further and complicate everything?

Our sister's suicide made us all feel guilty. That's the worst thing a suicide does to you. From the grave, she can make you care too much. "You just never did enough, did you?" says that wicked, merciless voice in your head. Couldn't you read the signs? Why weren't you there for her? These all end, of course, in the inevitable, You couldn't stop her, could you? No, none of us could stop her.

Asleep the night my sister died, hours before my sister-in-law called, I woke up with a jolt as my sister burst into the room with incredible energy. I heard her voice. I saw her, and then she was gone. I sat up in bed wondering what had just happened. I'd had a dream about my sister, but how strange! I hadn't dreamed about her, at least not that I could remember, for ten years or so. That I dreamed of her that night was extraordinary—until I got my sister-in-law's call a few hours later. Then it made chilled-to-the-bone sense.

"She came to say goodbye," my surviving sister said. Yes, but wouldn't a simple phone call have worked out better for everyone? Even hitchhiking her way to Indiana would have suited me more than the flight she booked on Astral Air. Why weren't you there for her?

How long does that litany of self-criticism go on? For some, it plays for the rest of their lives. For me, twenty years had to pass before I'd grown enough, learned enough and acquired the unwavering strength to reassess my sister's death.

There was no signature moment that led to my change of heart. As a father, I still find it hard to understand the trauma my sister inflicted on her children. I know her children endured terrible times after her death, but today they're all grown up and successful in their lives, with thriving families of their own. I wish my sister was around to see that, but I no longer judge her for not being here. I'm not wise enough or smart enough or right enough in my own life to judge her.

My change of heart also turns away from my more recent Buddhist training. Buddhists frown on suicide and mercy killings as interference with fate and karma. But once I was able to look from the vantage point of many years at my sister's passing, I noticed a key fact I'd missed or ignored at the time. When my freshly dead sister zoomed two thousand miles cross-country to wake me up moments after she died, she startled me and confused me, but the strongest impression I have of the experience today is this: she was happy. She was beautifully energized. She was happy! How she could have been, given the circumstances, I can't say. Even now, I can't be sure or do much more than speculate. But I am certain about the energetic quality she brought to my room that night. She had come to me and gone in a burst of dazzling light and power. She was liberated. She was free, and I like to think she was going home. Twenty years after my sister's death, I was able to write a poem of reconciliation.

Elegy in August

Sleep, little sister, far from pain.

Water polishes stones in the river

As memory calms the chaos

You left behind. Rest easy, sister,

Your babies are older than you ever were.

Even the stain will fade

When none are left to remember

The calls for help you never made.

After burning, blackberry bushes

Struggle up through ask, just as love, resilient,

Blooms in all seasons, even for you

Who suffered and could not tell what was right

As you hurled yourself, suddenly

Spiraling, upward to darkness or light.

It's not always so easy for the rest of us. Fr. Pat said once at the end of his best homily ever, "There is no hell, and heaven is here. This place. Right now." When the best dog I ever knew died, we grieved as if we'd lost a beloved family member, which we had. He was our Familiar. Being an animal, he had the advantage of a closer working relationship with the natural world, which he tried to teach us, and we got better at it the longer we lived together.

The ten years we had with him were not enough. Yet the energy continues on. He was a musical dog who learned to sing by listening to an old Jeanette MacDonald 78 disc we had. He would lean against a speaker with a dreamy, lovesick look on his face, incline his head back, and howl in tune during certain segments. Later on, we could set off his singing by giving a little howl.

He would launch into joyful, memorable arias that especially broke up the boredom of long car trips.

After his death, we only half joked that our second son was that dog reincarnated. He was born nine months after our dog's death, so our son never really knew him. But imagine the thrill and chill that ran up and down our spines, when one day in the kitchen at age five, our boy threw back his head and spontaneously howled a melody we knew so well and hadn't heard for years.

Outwardly, we didn't make too much of it, but inwardly we were awed and changed. That's what being attuned to life's (and death's) energy will do to you. There is an interesting coda to this anecdote. That child is in college now, a music major studying to be an opera singer.

Establishing and nurturing a relationship with an animal or animals always helps me immensely, especially during periods of grief. We're all energy beings, but adult humans easily forget this truth we all know so well in childhood. Guileless, animals tune into us with perfect honesty and immediacy. Animals invented being in the moment. If you are truly with an animal, you can't help but be grounded, centered, focused, and at ease.

"The best thing for the inside of a person is the outside of a horse," Will Rogers said once, but he might have said it about any animal.

In addition to the good company of animals, reading poems helped me cope with grief, too. Poems are our birth, love, and death songs. When we yearn for spiritual connection, we hunger for the sense and music of poetry. When we pray, we're speaking poems.

What we need and crave and spend our lives making and finding is our interconnected, rich, and varied stories. You are important. I am important. Together, we matter so much. We matter so much that our shared energy, our connection, does not end with the simplicity of death; it just becomes something else. This truth becomes plain enough the more you write through your grief, the more you dance with it and sing with it.

Sitting down in a sea of grief to write about grief is a sure way to transform your grief. Writing is the act of harvesting the green change in you after suffering. "After great pain a formal feeling comes," Emily Dickinson wrote, articulating with characteristic precision the place we get to after we've been broken by others or by circumstance. That formal feeling is wisdom. It's serenity, a calm acceptance of the Here and Now. It's also forgiveness.

Do you believe a doctor misdiagnosed or mistreated your departed loved one? Did you lose a job because your boss persecuted you? Did a sitter's inadequate care cause the death of your family pet? Go ahead! Write about these villains. Don't cut them any slack. In your writing, punch them! Take all the time you need. Just let them have it. Vent!

And when you have done it well, when your righteousness and vitriol are quite spent, breathe deeply and begin to write as if you are the person you've been impaling to walls and doors. Sound impossible? Just earnestly try it, and you'll be amazed at how readily you can write from that foreign point of view. In no time, it won't seem so foreign, and you'll notice something else. You'll experience a sea change in your heart as you feel more compassion for your enemy. It's the most amazing thing! Writing is witnessing, and it's confession. Writing is also empathy. When you're balanced, you'll feel and see and hear both sides of any conflict.

Without laughter, without poems, without journal entries, sacred places, and the animals that have watched over me, I'm not sure I would have come to this truth: I'll survive anything this sweet world throws at me. I can forgive anyone, and I know that any loss, no matter how painful, is alchemical and temporary.

About the Author

Robert McDowell is a poet, performer, storyteller, public speaker, educator and author of sixteen books including *Poetry as Spiritual Practice*. His latest book of poems is *The World Next to This One*. He has performed at the United Nations in Geneva with Dr. Rama Mani and elsewhere, sharing poems and stories focusing on gender issues and violence against women throughout history. His poems, stories, essays, and reviews have appeared in hundreds of anthologies and periodicals, including *Best American Poetry, Poetry, London Magazine, The New Criterion, Sewanee Review,* and *The Hudson Review.* He was the Co-Founder and Publisher of Story Line Press for twenty-two years. As a lifelong mentor of emerging poets, he has particularly championed women in print, literacy and women's rights. Website: robertmcdowell.net

The Power of Choices

Irit Oz

"You have the power to heal your life, and you need to know that. We think so often that we are helpless, but we're not. We always have the power of our minds . . . Claim and consciously use your power."
—Louise Hay

I woke up with an excruciating pain in my back. I couldn't even get out of bed. After lying there a while, I really needed the restroom. I had no choice, so I called to my husband, explaining the state I was in and allowing him to pick me up and carry me to the bathroom. I felt deeply ashamed as my husband lifted me with both hands and all his heart and carried me to the bathroom.

Then he carried me straight to the doctor's office.

After a blood test and back x-rays, the doctor informed me that my immune system was not working correctly and that I also had extreme inflammation. He prescribed antibiotics and told me to rest.

A week later, he performed the tests again to see if I had improved, but the results actually showed that the condition had worsened!

The next Friday as I got ready for work, I was relieved that it was a short day and I only had to work until 1 p.m. I was becoming completely fatigued, and as I approached the stairs leading to the parking lot, my feet got extremely painful. I knew it would have been impossible to climb them, so I went back home.

The following Sunday, I started the day on my feet, but finished it sitting in a wheelchair. I was about to finish a course I was taking to help children living in poor families. The class was only two hours long, but my legs swelled up and became painful. I couldn't concentrate, but I tried to collect myself and reconnect with the class. I grit my teeth and when it finally ended, I turned to my friend and asked, "Can you help me up? I can't get up on my own, and I can barely walk."

Hanging off my friend's shoulders on the way to the elevator, I felt severe pain and couldn't lift my legs. I thought this could only be very bad news. I can't lift my feet! What's happening to me?"

My friend helped me get into the car and home. I sat in the middle of my kitchen and realized that I had no choice. It was time to go to the hospital and find out what was happening. I told my husband, "I need to be admitted; I am not well."

My husband looked at me and nodded in agreement. When my mom arrived to look after my son, I realized that this was it. There is no way back, and I was stepping into the unknown.

That night I found myself lying motionless in bed with sore feet and dressed in hospital attire. Fear looked me in the eyes, and I looked at it. I felt our eyes lock, and we were both silent.

Over the next few weeks, the doctors performed every possible test on me, including an MRI, a CT scan, daily blood tests, cardio pulmonary exercises, stress tests, leg muscle tests, biopsies, etc....

Finally one of the doctors asked me to come unaccompanied into another room. I exchanged a worried look with my husband as I slowly rolled my wheelchair towards the room, feeling my nervousness getting the better of me.

Inside was a circle-shaped desk with eight doctors sitting around it looking extremely busy as they shuffled through what seemed to be copies of my medical file. No one would make eye contact with me, and the room was filled with a chilling silence. I wanted to shout, "God, somebody say something! I want to get this over and done with and go somewhere else."

One doctor fiddled with the paper and said, "Your situation is not good, and we can't really say what happened to you. We have diagnosed three different diseases you are suffering from: sarcoidosis, chronic fatigue syndrome, and potentially muscular dystrophy."

Another physician added, "Unfortunately with muscular atrophy disease, the typical life expectancy is, at most, ten years."

I listened to the barrage of unfamiliar words, disease names, explanations, and a worrying amount of uncertainty from the doctors. I sat in a wheelchair in front of a group of doctors feeling that I was freefalling down a cliff and into an icy pool, hitting my body on everything on the way down. I felt lonely and lost.

The doctors went on to explain, "The only known remedy that we know of that can help this condition is to administer huge amounts of cortisone over the course of a year, which would gradually decrease, depending on the way your body responds."

A quick and elusive thought passed through my head. If I had brought those diseases upon myself, then I should also be able to get rid of them! I didn't give this thought much attention, but looking back on it, I can tell you it represented a huge insight, and it saved my life.

Sitting helpless in the wheelchair surrounded by the doctors, I also remembered that my mother had experienced taking cortisone in the past. It nearly destroyed her, and I remembered her suffering.

I immediately refused to accept the treatment, and I asked for a treatment that would be less aggressive on my body. Despite my request, the doctors unanimously declared, "This is the only treatment we recommend!"

The room fell silent, and the doctors waited to hear my answer. I wasn't even sure I had the right to refuse at that point, but I did. Almost without hesitation, I repeated, "I will not take this poison into my body!"

When the doctors understood that this was my final decision, they asked that I go over to the table to sign a form which stated that I refused to accept their treatment recommendation. The document absolved the hospital of any responsibility for my health, and the responsibility fell solely on me.

I was discharged from the hospital without truly understanding what was going on, how I had gotten sick, or what I was going to do next.

For several weeks I lay in a special bed provided to me. I just lay there without a purpose, staring into space, feeling my sore legs, dead tired, overwhelmed, suppressing emotions, confused, self-absorbed, and detached from anything around me. I really had no strength to hear anything, much less say anything.

I finally underwent an examination to determine for sure whether or not I had muscular dystrophy. The neurologist said that I didn't have it! Yesssss! Yet, the inexplicable muscle weakness in my legs continued.

Then one day my friend's mother brought a man over to see me. She said, "Irit, this is Gal. He's the therapist I was telling you about. He wants to help you."

Gal talked to me about my situation, explaining something about water and fire. I did not really get it because I was mostly crying from the pain in my legs. Gal was massaging my feet, and it was excruciating. I cried and begged him to stop. He did and said, "You are the only one who can choose. I'm here to help you. When you choose, call me and I will come here, to your home, to help you. You choose, and I will be here!"

What? What the hell was he saying? What was there to choose between? How was this related to my condition? All I could think about was how much he had just hurt me. I just want everything to stop and everyone to leave me alone!

Later, I did choose, and Gal became my guardian angel. He came to my house three times a week, treating me with all his heart, understanding my suffering. He didn't give-in to me or give-up on me.

After three months of Gal's treatment, I began to stagger to my feet.

After five months, I was really starting to walk! Soon enough, I began travelling twice a week to Gal's clinic for more treatment. During the next two and a half years, when I was sick and in a bad place both physically and mentally, Gal was my guardian angel, continuously supporting me. He helped me grow stronger and stronger and didn't let me fall back.

About that time I went to the doctor for a routine check-up. He reviewed my recent medical tests and said, "Irit, you're pregnant."

I was stunned! Me? Pregnant? I had no idea! This was another sign I was not fully present in my own life.

The bad news was that they recommend I undergo an abortion, otherwise I would endanger myself and my baby's health and normal development. He said the hormonal changes that would take place during the pregnancy could inflame the disease. If that happened, then I would have to take the cortisone to come to full term, and that would harm the baby. He could be born with any number of maladies, such as a cleft lip.

He sent me home for the weekend saying I had to call back when I had decided on a course of action.

I immediately became emotionally attached and loved what I had in my womb! I stroked my little belly lovingly and knew, then and there, that I was not giving up this child. I was already giving and receiving love and intuitively knew that this pregnancy was important and meaningful!

"I have decided," I informed the doctor when I called. "I'm keeping my child."

I found myself, once again, signing a waiver acknowledging the doctor's warning about both my health and that of my unborn child.

A magical child came into my world following this pregnancy. I gave birth to a healthy, amazing, smiling child; a real sweetie with a pure soul with a birth given sense of values! Today, my divine child is already 16 years old; beautiful, with a heart of gold. He gives me nothing but pleasure, a sense of joy, and I feel privileged to accompany him throughout the years.

The pregnancy boosted my physical, mental, emotional, and spiritual wellbeing. I no longer felt tired and exhausted. My heart was joyful. I realized life had given me another chance to live it to the fullest. And this time I was not going to miss out!

Today, after many years of reflecting back, I ask what I have learned about myself. What wisdom did I gain? What am I doing differently? I recognize that my primary learning is mostly about my power as a person to choose. I've learned that even when I thought I had no power and death was knocking at my door, even then, we have a lot of power!

There were a few stops along the way, and in those places I stopped to listen to my heart and make choices based on what it said to me. When I drew upon my unwavering strength and took action using the gifts I've received, I experienced the most significant leaps in my journey.

Today, using a methodology I was inspired and chose to create, I help children, parents, families, and leaders in the business world.

This is what I do; this is who I am. I am so ecstatic when I see people I've touched becoming happier, more aware, more confident, and loving themselves more. I am happier and more fulfilled than ever before.

And I don't take my life for granted any longer either. I am extremely grateful that I got to this moment, because in this moment I'm grateful, in all my heart, for the goodness I earned by making difficult choices in my life.

I thank myself first, for being brave enough to make the choices that led me here. But I didn't do it all alone. I also want to thank my husband, my two wonderful sons, my gorgeous girl, my business partner, and my parents and family. I'm also grateful to Judy and to you, dear readers. And mostly, I thank God and the universe we live in.

I have the power to choose. We all do. And one by one, day by day, the choices we make create our lives.

In conclusion

Every time I skip up the stairs I remember that just a few years ago, I wasn't sure that I would be able to do that ever again. I will never forget what I experienced but my dream during that painful time—to walk, jump and run—is now fulfilled daily! I will always remember that it is because I chose not to give up that I am healthy today!

About the Author

Irit was born and raised in Tel Aviv, Israel. She started her professional career at the age of 18 as a communication instructor in the Israeli army (Where she received an Honorable Mention). After an experience of a serious illness, she turned to the education field. She started as an informal teacher for "interpersonal communication" and "how to learn." After one year she was appointed to be in charge of all diagnosis for children in the school and from there she became a personal coach and a super-nanny. In the last 14 years Irit has taught, coached, and mentored hundreds of people in countless walks of life. In 2013 Irit co-founded OZ & Hirshfeld Inc. a firm that specializes in Employee Engagement. The firm has a base in Tel Aviv and in the Silicon Valley, and through it; Irit is offering her knowledge and experience to organizations around the world. http://OzAndHirshfeld.com

Love Is All

Alice Theriault

"I had you and I have you no more, Oh, little words, how can you run so straight across the pages, beneath the weight you bear?"
—Edna St. Vincent Millay

How do I convey in mere words love that transcends all time and life experiences, all wrenching of the heart? How do I gather the essence of existence, the pith, core and marrow, and see what remains? The answer is simple: through unwavering strength, for love is all.

This is the life journey of my son Brett. Seemingly tragic and burdensome, his walk culminated with a quantum leap in the evolution of his soul and mine. This is not a personal lament upon the sadness of his life, but a testimony to the poignant beauty of his spirit.

The Good Book says all things work together for good to those who love God and are called according to God's purpose. We came from love. We are beings of love, which is the infinite expression of God, Divine Presence, Great Spirit, The Absolute, or whatever is your choice for the source of all being.

That which calls us into form is both God's purpose and our purpose, so easily forgotten as we become immersed in the physical aspects of life. However, our purpose in form, in our bodies, is the enlightenment and evolution of our eternal souls. Hildegard of Bingen, a 12th century mystic, said, "Within the cosmic order of things, humankind (we who contain within ourselves the elements both of heaven and earth) represents a central mediating point located between the divine and the earthly. Our own nature—the rhythms of our minds and bodies, are an echo of the rhythms of the natural world. We do not exist in isolation, but are parts of an encompassing whole."

I believe that we choose our parents and the blueprint of circumstances that we need to develop at a soul level. Therefore, an arduous path can ultimately reveal and create love and goodness throughout the many lives affected by it. Life is a beautiful web of interconnectedness and oneness; uplifting and assisting all.

My son's legacy is for us to understand and comprehend life's purpose with the beginning—and also the ending—as part of a great cycle of the one eternal life, the life of Spirit, which he so clearly demonstrated in his beautifully tragic lifetime.

I was blessed on November 12, 1963, with the arrival of my third child, a perfect baby boy. He arrived in a flurry of frantic moments, twenty minutes to be exact, leaving me breathless. And breathless I remained throughout his life.

We bonded immediately, and from the moment he was laid upon my tummy, I knew he had a special love to call forth from life, a destiny, if you will. Our connection was very deep, and we communicated with our eyes and thoughts. I could only smile at him and with him and found it difficult to scold or be annoyed with his antics. He was a beautiful blue-eyed boy with a softness about him, yet a typical boy, pounding on everything, climbing over the fence at sixteen months, and many other "monkey shines!"

When Brett was two years old, I wrote a poem as love welled up in my heart for this incredible blessing, toddling around smiling at me, a wet grin revealing his chipped front tooth that was the first of many, many boo-boos. I had no idea at the time that it would prove to be prophetic.

My darling boy with eyes of blue,

Oh, that I could live for you,

All the chaos, pain and strife,

Part and parcel of ephemeral life.

But alas, would my gift,

Serve to set your soul adrift,

Without the tenacity to revere,

The joy of life while you are here?

The "chaos, pain and strife" lay in wait for us, but life unfolded as it will. The early years were normal, save the unusual behavior of nightly restlessness with rocking and roaming. Occasionally I would be awakened by this small being standing over me! He was full of energy and life and seldom still. In spite of these childhood concerns, he was a dear child of incredible sweetness and love. In retrospect, I now understand the restlessness. He was suffering with tummy rumblings he could not explain to me at the time.

At age eight stomach aches became increasingly frequent and severe. After a doctor visit and diagnosis of colitis, the pattern continued. At age nine a severe episode prompted exploratory surgery, and Brett was diagnosed with Crohn's Disease, a chronic inflammatory process affecting the entire intestinal system. He was given Prednisone, an anti-inflammatory steroid that has many side effects and is difficult to tolerate. I read everything I could find searching for a solution but to no avail. Our lives became complicated with the ups and downs of difficult treatments, hospitalizations, surgeries, pain and stress.

My heart was now aching, heavy with my boy's pain,

The sun will come up, a new trial will begin—I am not ready.

It was here I wrote the following poem as I drove home from the hospital after yet another bowel closure episode, with nasal gastric tubes and pain.

Pursuit

I long for days of my newness,

When life lay ahead like a bright bubble waiting to be captured,

Now I struggle in days of my oldness

And mist from the shattered bubble

Has dampened my spirit for the chase.

Brett's first surgery, a re-section, the removal of a diseased portion of the small bowel, was performed when he was eleven years old with hope that the frequent flare-ups would be eliminated, but they continued. The bowel at the surgery site was compromised, weakened and resulted in more pain, infections, and more complications. Here is where the plot thickens, as they say.

Three horrendous nightly bowel closure episodes, each two weeks apart, tore at my heart and Brett's precious body. My religious faith at the time was to ask for healing (actually beg), as I believed God would not want him to suffer. But we were suffering, just as were many others.

After the third obstruction came with no healing in sight, I knew that I could no longer ask to have this pain removed, and only asked that it be glorified in our lives with the strength to withstand it. In other words, ask God for help to deal with it, not just to take it away. I remember my words: Show me how to do this.

Faith and unwavering strength were the answers to withstand any trial, and all that was needed was to knuckle down, continue prayers, and tap into the ability to remain strong and supported, no matter what (or NMW, as I titled it). Was this a test? Is this what faith means? If so, then what is religion for? How do I survive the pain of this child's experience so tragically enmeshed with mine? Confusion reigned. I buckled (no unwavering strength here), and I was a mess!

> *"Life must go on; I forget just why."*
> —Edna St. Vincent Millay

I, the one responsible for my son's welfare, now questioned everything about life, religion, spirituality, and how to combine it all with chronic illness. My faith in a higher power was greatly tested as I struggled with daily illness and family adjustments. I knew that somehow I must be able to deal with our desperate situation.

As I revisit that time, I believe my search for solutions and answers was a way of opening me to my own strengths, a way of coming closer and more in tune with Spirit. When life presents a problem, we must confront it, not go over or around it, but through it! Planted firmly in our path, it is part of the whole life experience, regardless of how it is perceived on a physical level. This is where I had to connect with my true purpose in the body, the elusiveness that was holding me captive. I knew we are all part of the whole and each life impacts others. If life gives us lemons, we make lemonade. At least we do after we get our ducks in a row and realize that all things work together for good.

We are meant to live gloriously, to love and serve others, and remember who we truly are; spiritual beings with physical experiences. Our Source is greater than we can imagine, with the wisdom needed to be the best we can be, in spite of the challenges. We lie within the very heart of God. We are the life force, and therein is the power to bring about the greater good. It is written, "Ye are Gods, and all of ye are children of the Most High."

It seems quite clear that we are here with divine purpose and no less. So, as we step up to the plate with each new opportunity to become that which we already are, we are armed from on high and must remember, remember,

remember. The word *remember* truly means to re-member; to bring together scattered pieces of ourselves due to physical incarnation, forgotten pieces that were always there, our spiritual heritage. These truths remain our very armor and breastplate, our unwavering strength, which equals divine love in every sense of the word.

As a child, Brett identified with the biblical story of Job because his faith was tested with many trials. Throughout his life, even as a child, Brett experienced Spirit in many forms, including visitations in dreams from angels and spiritual masters. Upon awakening from an induced coma while in the hospital, he repeated the phrase, "Nobody dies; nobody dies."

In his final months he was visited by Archangel Raphael, the angel of healing forces, standing at the foot of his hospital bed dressed in battle gear. It was on that day that I sang the divine Buddhist mantra, Öm Mani Padme Hum, to comfort him. We shared love and gratitude with each other for our continuing poignant connection. I believe he was a spiritual master here to spread his wings and endure his own special piece of world karma.

After being hospitalized for five months, Brett passed on at age thirty-nine due to severe debilitation of his body wracked with Crohn's Disease. He remained in communication with angels and spoke openly to me about them. At the end, his immune system completely failed. Incisions from his last surgery could not heal, and there was no choice but to allow the bleeding out of his precious body. It was divinely peaceful as friends and family gathered and sent love and last wishes. He could not respond as a tracheotomy had silenced his voice, but when I asked if he was in pain he moved his head to indicate no.

The love we shared sets a life-sized example of unwavering strength. My last words to him as his life's blood dripped upon my shoes were, "Thank you for being my teacher. I love you beyond love."

The body upon the bed was just a shell, and realization as big as life, literally, was upon me: Spirit is all, and Spirit is love.

Great love is unwavering strength. Love is all. And so it is.

About the Author

Alice Theriault is a retired elementary teacher with thirty year's experience. She is a reverend in the Universal Church of the Master, a poet, a member of the National League of American Pen Women and the author of a newly published book, *Take Hold of Heaven, Thirteen Spiritual Truths for Parents and Children*. She is a mother of five, grandmother of ten, great-grand-mother of three and a lover of planet Earth and all creation. She resides in San Jose, California with a bevy of family, three cats, a hamster, and two fish (www.takeholdofheaven.com).

Calamity, Alchemy, and the Power of Laughter

Faith Poe

"I contend that not only can you laugh at adversity, but it is essential to do so if you are to deal with setbacks without defeat."
—Allen Klein

My friend Jessie is a petite, physically fit, and perfectly toned natural red head. Several years ago, she described her blissful childhood. Her parents remain happily married. Financially successful, she lives her passion. She never experienced any major traumas and commented how blessed she feels.

Unlike Jessie, I am not petite, physically fit or toned, and my red hair is courtesy of my hairdresser. My life spins in the opposite direction from Jessie's. I often find myself desperately clinging by my fingertips to keep from flying off into a chasm of no return. No matter where I roam, work, travel or play, misadventures seem to follow. Fasten your seat belts for a whirlwind ride on the Calamity Express as I chronicle some of the catastrophes that I have experienced.

Throughout my action-filled years, I managed to find myself taking too many turns down accident alley. My childhood dream of soaring high in the sky in a hot air balloon certainly did not include hurling to the ground as we crashed into the desert. While visiting a boyfriend in Washington, D. C., the ice-covered road became the ideal setting when our car came in second and we found ourselves in a ten-car pile up. My twenty year cruise ship career provided countless unexpected twists. Catapulted out of bed onto the floor while cruising from Istanbul to Athens, I awoke to the terrifying discovery we shipwrecked onto an unscheduled island port of call.

The heart-crushing pain remains after losing loved ones to murder, suicide, accidents, and illness. A different heartache ensued after two not-so-happily-ever-after marriages ended in divorce.

My catalog of catastrophes lists multiple entries as "crime victim." After sightseeing all day in Los Angeles with friends, six ski-masked robbers, dressed head-to-toe in black, greeted us upon the return to our host's home. With not one, but two guns to my head, fear gripped me stronger than the fingers on their triggers as they robbed us and held us for hours. A hotheaded Greek, a total stranger, angrily beat me up by pounding my head into the wall inside a jewelry store on that romantic, picturesque street in Santorini you see in travel magazines.

I ended up in the center of two riots that made national headlines. In Atlanta, police teargased us when a free concert in the park abruptly ended due to conflicts. Fires encircled the apartment where I stayed with a friend during the L.A. riots years later. Neither provoked riotous laughter.

Enter the epidemics. Legionnaires Disease broke out on a ship that cruised weekly from New York to Bermuda. Several people died and most of us fell ill. While living in Cozumel, Mexico, Swine Flu impacted islanders in unexpected ways, even though no one contracted the disease.

For many years, I suffered extreme anxiety every time I flew, to the point of needing medication. Once, a traveling companion asked why I was so afraid, considering how much I traveled by air. I know 13 people who have immediate family members who died in plane crashes, including my father. I know no one who has died in a car crash.

Doctors sliced me as much as Geppetto carved Pinocchio in surgeries that included an emergency appendectomy after a year of undiagnosed and unrelated illnesses, and the not-so-exotic surgery for skin cancer on my face after it appeared that an alien grew out of it.

Although I have plenty of nutty friends, I knocked on death's door on multiple occasions due to a peanut allergy, including once on a transatlantic flight. Resembling Violet Beauregarde in Willy Wonka, I swelled with 70 additional pounds in a year. Not until many years later, doctors diagnosed a thyroid issue due to medication taken for severe depression in my 20's. Though my body did not turn blue, my mood most certainly did.

After various calamities, I sent out prayers pleading *"Please, dear God, give me a break!"*

I got a break all right, in fact too many to count. After losing consciousness in a scooter accident in Jamaica, I came around in time to hear the doctor say, *"Don't let her see a mirror,"* followed by *"Young lady, I think you have broken every bone in your face."* My first (and last) ski trip resulted in a broken leg in Vail, Colorado. And while leading a tour in Mexico, I fell and cracked several teeth which led me to a horrifying experience with a Serial Driller. No, I was not wearing stilettos. I have a talent for falling off flats. Another face plant in Barcelona required my front teeth to be replaced once again. But my missing teeth did help my Castilian accent as I lisped along the painful trip home.

No stranger to natural disasters, I have first hand experience with several. Cruise ships periodically go into dry dock in order to remodel the ship and check it out head to toe. Docked in Freeport, Bahamas, the unpredicted first-ever tornadoes hit our ship and killed several people across the dock as they worked in a crane. While visiting San Francisco with friends in the 80s, we found ourselves in the middle of the financial district during a 6.9 earthquake.

I managed to get out on the last flight leaving Cozumel before the strongest hurricane recorded in the Atlantic churned over the island as a Category 5 for 55 hours. Unable to return for six weeks, I stayed with friends in Florida before going back to face the devastation. The storm ripped fans out of the ceiling, closet doors from the hinges, and they found my refrigerator from my forth floor apartment in the stairwell on floor three. What little remained were piles of damaged and unrecognizable items in heaps across the floor. Wilma's forceful vacuum sucked out all of my possessions along with my spirit. A better name for this hurricane would have been Hurricane Hannibal.

Next came an avalanche of adversity as a result of this forceful beast. The owner of the condo I purchased pre-construction turned out to be a crook. Against my attorney's advice to walk away and cut my losses, I thought since I was in the right, I would fight the fight. The next year of legal battles threw me into an emotional tail spin. Once they presented forged documents in court, I not only lost the condo, but also had to pay their attorney fees as an exclamation point to my sentence. Totally defeated, I lost my personality and perspective, unable to recognize my angry alter ego. I contracted shingles, 100% from stress, with an unrelenting pain that felt like burning acid with needles being poked into my skin. Business suffered and I lost the career I loved, only to be followed by the economic meltdown that now matched my own. Permanent employment leads remained illusive, as I survived on random consulting jobs. Wiped out financially by this time, I suffered a serious spiritual crisis.

After Hurricane Wilma wiped out life as I knew it, I conducted my own life review. I recalled all of the calamities I experienced and how my life screeched to a halt following each disaster. Overwhelmed with fear, grief, complete loss of confidence, and most significantly isolation, the depths of various misfortunes incapacitated me in ways I could not imagine. After much reflection, I realized that various traumas affected me in more than one area of my life. Wilma affected all areas including my emotional and physical health, finances, career, relationships, and my spiritual connection. Two things provided unwavering strength and allowed me to prevail over even the most precarious misadventures: gratitude and laughter. Those practices grant remarkable freedom, empowering me to LOL (Leap Out of Loss) and back into life.

L. **Laughter** always opens a space to change the perspective on my many challenges.

A. **Alchemy** is my practice of transmuting an unbearable event that cannot be changed into an amusing look back in order to move forward.

U. I find **Uplifting** ways to change my outlook by watching funny movies or short YouTube videos that made me laugh out loud.

G. **Gratitude** keeps me in a state of appreciation in the darkest of times. I count my blessings throughout each day.

H. Although I did not laugh at the time I came up against each calamity, once able to find the absurdity and **Humor** in each setback, the tragedy lost its grip on me. I no longer re-live the traumas, I merely re-tell them.

About the Author

Author Faith Poe, the Calamity Alchemist, is truly an expert when it comes to the one thing she'd rather not be known for: Disasters! Not studying them, but tumbling through them to discover the absurdity on the other side. She believes that although she cannot avoid misfortune, she can choose to live in her stories or laugh her way through them and celebrate at the other end. She has enjoyed a marketing and lecturing career in the always-unpredictable cruise-ship industry for over two decades. Born in the desert town of El Paso, Texas, Faith is an avid traveler. She enjoyed nine years of island life while living in Cozumel in the winters and Alaska in the summers. She holds degrees in Journalism and Photography/Film in addition to a Masters in Disasters and an M.D. in Laughter, the best medicine. She is the author of the forthcoming book: *Calamity Cocktails: Shaken and Stirred by Twists of Fate (www.CalamityCocktails.com).*

Half-Step Back

Tracy Friesen

"You gain strength, courage, and confidence by every experience in which you really stop to look fear in the face. You must do the thing which you think you cannot do."
—Eleanor Roosevelt

This story covers the very thing we are most afraid of losing—our ability to survive.

Four years ago my husband of fifteen years and I went through a separation. It wasn't the nasty kind that you hear about, it was just what it was—a separation. Although, you may think, "Big deal!" for me it was the hardest decision I ever had to make and the hardest thing I ever had to do. This wasn't about someone else—this was about me. Once I began to realize the consequences of my decisions, I became concerned about what my future would be like. I could be about to throw my life into chaos and I had to muster the courage and the strength to have a serious reality check. It wasn't about not loving him, it was that my happiness became more important. This decision did not come lightly nor did it come from a lacking of trying as my husband and I did a number of things to see how we could repair the distance. Nothing stuck. All the scary questions started to haunt me from the moment I woke until I went to bed again. Who gets the house? Who gets what? Where will I live? Where will he live? Where will our daughter live? Are we going to fight for custody? Will this be amicable? Can we afford this? Oh my goodness, can I survive?

With all these frightening and daunting questions floating around like elephants in the room, my husband and I still had to make these decisions and the next few weeks were not fun, to say the least. Through months of difficult days of trying to accept that what I was doing was the right thing, I finally found a place to live that met my basic needs. When I moved in, the reality of my situation finally sunk in. An overwhelming fear over took me and I fell to the floor and cried uncontrollably.

My story begins about a week after I moved into my own place, and I had yet to go to sleep with the lights off.

As a Certified Energy Medicine Practitioner I know how to interact with people and their energy so I had signed up for a program to learn how to do the same with animals. Animals do not have filters, so just like a child, they will tell you like it is. In this training course I knew I was going to be working with horses, and since I had a fear of being around them, I thought this would be the best way for me to be able to get in touch with that fear.

I attended the Friday evening introduction with apprehension in my heart. I did not allow myself to get comfortable with these horse people. I say horse people because everyone in the room was completely comfortable being around horses, and I was completely out of my element. I felt fearful. I didn't feel safe.

After the session, I stuck around a bit to talk to the instructor. We talked about how troubled I felt about my life, and I finally left around midnight. As I left, I was overwhelmed with fear when I saw my car parked all the way across the dark, looming farmyard. It seemed like an endless trek as every hair on my body began to stand on end.

The only light was from a single bulb high on a wooden post, which created an eerie and ominous boundary that you could not see beyond. It was pitch black, and by the time I got to my car, my hands were shaking so badly that I had trouble getting the key in the door.

I drove away in a panic at speeds not meant for the shifting gravel. I called a friend just to have a sense that someone was with me, and when I got home, I don't think you'll be surprised to know that I did not sleep with the lights off this particular night either.

On Saturday, because I was so afraid of horses, the owner assigned me to Root beer. Even though Root beer was just a pony, I was still afraid that somehow I was going to get trampled. He felt my fear, and I could not get him to do the simplest of things like stand still, move here, move there or anything else. A sense of failure sunk in, and I was feeling even more defeated.

Towards the end of the day, I managed to access my inner unwavering strength as a confident healer and Root beer appreciated the energy we were sharing. But I still felt beaten at the end of the day.

Coming back Sunday was extremely hard for me. I almost didn't go because of all the guilt, shame, embarrassment, insecurity and untrusting feelings I had. But after checking in I started to lighten up a bit, although fear was still gnawing at the frayed edges of my nerves.

When it was time to apply what we had learned, my teacher approached me with the only gentleman in the group. She asked me if I was open to working with Cliff for the afternoon. I regarded him with that menacing, foreshadowing feeling surrounding me, but I sheepishly answered, "I am open to allowing whatever shall be, and I would be honored to work with Cliff this afternoon."

My teacher told me that she was confident in my knowledge and techniques and just to be open to allow what may be there for me to experience. I looked at her with apprehension and, as scared as I was, headed out the door behind Cliff.

We walked past the barn towards the pens in the back, and I could just feel my fear building. There were two horses in the back corral. I hesitated at the gate until Cliff encouraged me to enter. He said, "You're alright. I'm here with you."

Then he said, "Tracy, you're going to be working with Beaver today." He continued, "But first come on over here to Badger. Don't worry, he's a gentle and loving horse and won't hurt you or anyone."

He showed me how to halter him then said it was my turn. Trembling, I approached Badger and clumsily got the halter on. I started to back away toward the gate, but Cliff said I had to do it again. With my hands shaking so badly, it took longer than the first time, but I eventually got the halter on again.

Cliff then asked his daughter to lead Badger out. I pressed my back against the fence because I was afraid of getting hurt. Cliff looked at me with kind eyes and said "Now you're going to do the same to Beaver."

I looked at Beaver, and terror gripped my insides! He was a huge mass of potential devastation. He said, "Beaver's different from Badger. Beaver doesn't trust anyone, and what we are going to do is break down that trust even more. And then you're going to have to build his trust before you halter him."

I felt like crying.

To break down Beaver's trust, Cliff asked me to walk aggressively towards him. "You want me to do WHAT?"

He saw my fear and offered to show me what he meant. He walked real fast and sternly towards Beaver, and he waved his arms a bit. When he got close, Beaver ran away.

He said, "Now you try it."

Terrified, I walked aggressively towards the massive animal. I didn't even take four steps before Beaver took off towards Cliff. Cliff realized that Beaver wouldn't do what he wanted him to do if he was in the corral with us, so he jumped out. I'm pretty sure I stopped breathing. Now, it was just this humungous, monstrous beast and me—alone—inside the pen. I felt like crying again and exclaimed, "Cliff, I don't think I can do this!"

Cliff assured me that if I listened to him and did everything he asked me to do I would be OK. So with my wavering strength and conviction to see this to the end, I settled in to what I was about to experience. Sometimes the only way out is through.

I mustered every bit of courage I had and charged toward Beaver, waving my hands in the air. Cliff said, "Ok, Tracy, what is Beaver doing?"

I stopped in my tracks and hollered back, "He's getting ready to attack me!"

Ever patient, Cliff asked again, "Tracy, when you are walking at him aggressively, what is he doing?"

"He's running away." I said, more softly now.

"Exactly!" he said, "That's what people do when you come at them with aggression. They run away! Now it's time to start building up trust with Beaver." He continued, "Now listen to me and do exactly as I say."

He asked me to walk at an angle towards Beaver's back hip, and when I felt his energy I was to stop. When I did, Beaver looked away from me but didn't move. Cliff directed me to connect energetically with Beaver and start telling him that I mean no harm.

"OK, Tracy," Cliff said, "Look up over his back end, take one step closer, and then look down."

I nervously did as I was told, and Cliff reminded me to continue to connect and reassure Beaver that only good will come from us working together.

We repeated this process, which seemed like an eternity, until I was about two steps away from Beaver's head. Suddenly Badger started to neigh out in the front yard. I could tell Beaver wanted to go, and I started to get nervous that he would take off.

Cliff said, "Tracy, do you see what is happening? Beaver wants to go be with his friend, but he isn't sure he wants to leave because of what you've created so far. If you take a step closer, Beaver will most likely leave."

He asked, "Tracy, can you see where you may have created this in your own life?"

I sucked in a breath as his point hit me right between the eyes.

He continued, "Now I want you to take a half step back and give Beaver his space so he can decide what he wants to do."

I started to cry, and as tears silently rolled down my face, I understood how I had contributed to the strife in my marriage. I had tried to force things to get better. Even though I knew I was coming from unconditional love and that only good would come from what I had to offer, I had failed to take a half step back to allow space for my husband to decide if he wanted to let me in.

After several moments Cliff said, "OK, Tracy, you can take a step closer now. When you feel like Beaver has given you permission, you can reach out and touch his shoulder."

I did, and it wasn't long before I was petting Beaver along his neck and shoulder. I was elated, and with Cliff's guidance, I was able to walk completely around the horse under his neck and back to my original spot. I felt like I had just performed some kind of death-defying feat! I was overjoyed!

Cliff told me that I could put on the halter, and Beaver lovingly allowed me to move with grace and confidence. I led him out of the corral, and we walked into the front yard, nothing between us but love, trust and faith.

Back in circle, I shared what had happened, and then Cliff added, "Tracy was completely terrified of horses this morning, but because we're all horse people, we can't even begin to understand what she accomplished."

He stood up and acted out this analogy, "Imagine that I am a lion tamer, and I asked you to go into the lion's cage, break down its trust, then rebuild it and then open up its mouth and stick your head in!" Everyone smiled and nodded as he continued; "Within a short period of time, Tracy was able to build enough trust with Beaver that he let her harness him and walk him out. Up until today, the only two people that have ever been able to harness Beaver have been myself and my daughter, that's huge!"

I was really proud of myself! Not only was I able to overcome my fear of horses, but I was also able to see how I had impacted other people in my life. I realized that sometimes we all need to take a half step back to allow others to decide if they want to accept our help and let us into their lives. It was in that moment that with my unwavering strength of seeing it through, I finally felt like everything was going to be OK and that I would survive. That night I slept like a baby in my new house . . . with the lights out.

About the Author

With a background in software development, Tracy is a Certified Energy Medicine Practitioner. She shares her lifetime of experiences through writing and coaching individuals in group and one-on-one sessions. She has helped many people manifest the life they have always dreamed of by releasing what isn't working for them any longer and discovering that in the end everything really is OK. Find Tracy on the web at www.TracyFriesen.com, on Facebook as RideTheWaves.Book and on Twitter as @_RideTheWaves.

The Power of Creative Capacity

Wendy Knight Agard

*"The ability to choose is our creative capacity that we are born with,
and no experience or person can rob us of that capacity."*
—Wendy Knight Agard

I t's a typical evening, and I'm falling asleep when I hear my parents come home from grocery shopping. For reasons I can't explain, I slip out of bed and find myself in the hallway. One of the grocery bags with toiletries is sitting there waiting to be unpacked. At the very top of the bag is a glossy package of Juicy Fruit gum. Mmmmm, my sensitive nose can smell it as I pick it up, and I think how good it would be to have some right now. I hear my inner voice say, "Do it! Take it! They won't notice that it's gone!"

Before you know it, I'm back in my bed chewing the delicious gum. Being the novice thief that I am, I hadn't thought this through. Where would I put the gum after I chewed it? The only solution seems to be to swallow it. Then I feverishly wonder where I will hide the rest of the pack. In my panic I decide the best solution is to chew and swallow the entire pack. So I fretfully eat all of it there in the dark, my younger sister asleep across the room, completely ignorant of my licentious deed.

A few minutes later my heart stops when my father opens my door and asks, "Wendy, I had some gum in this grocery bag. Did you see it?"

Gripped with the fear of getting caught, I manage to squeak out, "No."

I realize that my crime was incredibly foolish. Of course he would notice! This is my father, a man who operated in a highly organized world of military precision. I crumple the wrappers, bury them under some balls of facial tissue in the garbage can and finally fall asleep wrapped in crippling guilt and terrifying dread.

The next day I came home from school for lunch. My mother is standing at the front door as soon as I open it. Tapping a stick of Juicy Fruit in her palm, the look on her face says it all. I've never seen her look angrier. I'm busted.

She says, "I found this under your pillow this morning."

It is now evident that amidst all of that chewing and swallowing and burying wrappers in the dark, I had lost a piece in my bed. A wave of panic washes over me, and my legs go numb.

She says, "Just wait until your father gets home! You can tell him what you've done."

It's the end of the school day and the bell rings. This is probably the only time I can remember NOT wanting the school day to end. Somehow my legs that I haven't felt since noon carry me home.

I go straight to my room and wait for the major to come home for dinner. An eternity passes. And then, he's home. He's in his uniform. My mother says, "Wendy has something to tell you."

He knows from her tone that I've done something wrong, and he turns his sharp gaze to me. I look up at him and almost whisper, "Daddy, I stole your gum."

He peels off his wire-rimmed aviator sunglasses and slowly places them beside the change on the kitchen counter. His jaw sets and tightens, and I can feel his energy shift to a deep anger. He is furious. I can feel my mother's satisfaction as she concludes that the truth is out and now my dad would deal with me.

He says, "You lied, Wendy. I asked if you had seen it, and you said you hadn't."

I stand frozen in silent terror and wait for whatever will come next. He raises his voice and says that it's bad enough that I took the gum, but lying about it makes it far worse. He says that he will have his dinner, and then he will punish me.

I was required to clean my plate every night, so I dutifully ate whatever was on my plate. I am still in a stupefied state of fear and it feels like time and space have not moved since noon. My two older siblings are told to be present in the family room after dinner for the punishment. Everyone eats in silence, anticipating the event. My younger sister is too young to understand what is happening and seems oblivious to the tension. How I envy her.

And now it's time. Dinner is over. My older brother and sister are told to sit on the sofa, along with my mother. My father tells me to go get his belt. Ah, so it will be a strapping. I still can't feel my body as I mount the stairs, go to his room and move my hands through the various belts flung over a chair in his bedroom. Somehow I know which belt he wants. It's the one he wears most often when he's not at work. It's about 2 inches wide and its well-worn leather suddenly takes on a whole new meaning to me. I carry the heavy belt in my small hands down the upstairs hall, down the stairs, down the main floor hall, through the kitchen to where he is standing, waiting, in the middle of the family room. It is such a long, long walk.

I arrive in front of him, and he tells me to pull down my pants and underwear. The emotional nudity is far worse than the physical nudity. I feel exposed as the evil-doer that I have been led to believe I am. My behind is cold, and I am embarrassed to be standing there with my pants around my ankles, on display for my siblings and my mother. I am to be made an example for them in addition to receiving the punishment for my crime. Of course, they have seen me without clothing before, but this is a different kind of exposure. This is meant to punish, to belittle, and to shame.

Six hours of panic-stricken anticipation comes to an end and is replaced by searing, stinging pain. I am now acutely aware of my body for the first time since noon. I've been violently pulled out of my emotional stupor and forced squarely into the physical pain of the first strike. My emotions kick back in, and they're running wild as I anticipate each new blow. In a rage now, his strained voice reminds me of my crime with each blow. I try to twist away between each strike, but his huge hand grips my spindly bicep. My tears are flowing now. They have been frozen in time and space along with my terror until now.

There is no sound from the sofa. The three of them sit there as they were instructed to do and wait for it to end. I wrench my head around to catch my mother's eye as often as I can during the strapping, hoping that she will see the pleading in my eyes and step in. But her face is set like a stone, and there is no emotion radiating from her. Her eyes offer no empathy or support. She just sits.

Too many years later, I realize that something else just as harmful as the strapping happened that day. My child's mind falsely concluded that I was utterly and completely alone. I could never really trust anyone to be there for me, not my mother, not my father, not God, not the universe, not even myself. Somehow I managed to live with that false belief by immersing myself in the things I enjoyed, athletics, art, and music. The theme running through my interests was creativity. Even athletics felt creative to me because every game, every practice session, and every competition was unique. It never happened exactly the same way, so there was a creative process involved that I connected with.

I came to understand that this creative capacity within us is what allows us to overcome anything. We can rewrite a false belief system. We can create a different thought, feeling, or reaction. We can choose to have a past experience serve us in a productive way, even if that experience was traumatic at the time. This is my unwavering strength. It is your unwavering strength. It is engendered in every fiber of our being. We have that capacity simply because we exist.

Overcoming that false belief that I developed as a child has been a slow and steady journey. It's been a beautiful, creative process to know that I am loved and cared for simply because I AM.

About the Author

Wendy Knight Agard is an Everyday Genius™ and Doctor of Heilkunst Medicine who helps leaders ignite their personal brand of genius through coaching and speaking programs that create profound results at the physical, emotional and soul/spiritual levels. After a successful corporate career in various leadership positions, Wendy chose to follow her passion to help people create more happiness and peace in their lives. Her forthcoming book: *Everyday Genius: A Common Sense Guide to Peaceful Leadership,* shows leaders how to lead themselves and others with confidence and ease.

Wendy is the wife of an amazing husband, mother of two fabulous teenagers, and the chief neck scratcher of their fun-loving dog Cosmo. Connect with her at www.WendyKnightAgard.com.

Falling Into the Rhythm of Life

Life Lessons Straight from the Horse's Mouth

Sharon Campbell Rayment

"It's not how far you fall, but how high you bounce that counts."
—Zig Ziglar

D id you ever make one decision that would change your life forever? I did. It was on July 11, 2008. I was performing for parents of children who had attended my horseback riding camp, and I made the decision to pay more attention to the crowd than to Malachi, my horse. This is the story of my fall, what I've learned through my recovery, and the unwavering strength I have gained from the "great fall" that has made me so "grate-full."

There is one moment in time I will never forget. Falling through the air, I felt light, weightless, and suspended in time. My head slammed off the ground, and the force from the bounce after the first hit sent my body upright. My head, back and hips slammed against the cement-like ground over and over. Every strike was incredibly powerful, and it was as if a lightning bolt sent shocks through my body and roared throughout my skull.

I remember darkness, a peaceful midnight black, like a dark velvet curtain, and it enveloped me into a cocoon of silent stillness.

Slowly, I emerged from a dark abyss. I heard a voice calling my name and the sound of people crying. I sensed confusion around me, and waves of pain were shooting through my body.

"Why am I here?" I asked.

I heard a voice say, "You have fallen off your horse."

Then, the velvet darkness engulfed me again. "Why am I here?" I asked a second time.

"You have fallen off your horse," I'm reminded by a patient and soothing voice.

I could only utter the word "Oh" when the dark curtain fell around me for the third time, and again I slipped away from consciousness.

Then I saw my husband Doug standing beside the Stryker board that I was lying on. I felt a tingling sensation in the crown of my head that later descended throughout my body. I knew something was wrong, very wrong. I couldn't speak or move. I traveled in and out of consciousness, confused by two very different worlds that were oddly connected, one draped in velvety darkness and the other bright and surreal.

In the weeks that followed, I was disoriented. Ten days after the accident, I awoke, only to realize that I had lost my ability to speak. Echoes in my mind bounced thoughts back and forth, but I couldn't get my mind to release my thoughts or express them to others. I grew frustrated and disillusioned because I heard people asking me questions, but I couldn't answer.

Days turned into weeks, and weeks drifted into years. I flowed in and out of depression, sinking into the abyss for months. The woman I was before the accident had disappeared, and I desperately wanted her to return.

Before my fall, I was an active woman and ran general and special population horseback riding classes for five years. School groups visited my farm, and I taught horseback riding lessons and ran camps. As a pastor of a three-point charge, I also prepared a Sunday service for my 9:00 a.m., 10:15 a.m., and 11:30 a.m. services. I ran confirmation, baptismal, and wedding preparation sessions and visited members of my churches. I was a mother, wife, and friend who had received a Master of Divinity degree only six months before my fall.

After the fall, I would never again be able to keep up this pace, and it made me frustrated and quick tempered.

I no longer am able to tolerate noise and confusion, nor do I feel comfortable in a crowd. I am unable to commit to a schedule, and if you ask me to make a quick decision, I'll panic and appear confused. I am now introverted rather than extroverted. My life before the fall was multifaceted and sometimes disorganized. Now, disorganization upsets and confuses me.

My brain injury left me with Foreign Accent Syndrome. After the fall, I developed a wee Scottish brogue. I roll my r's, shorten my ing's, and think everything is grrraaannd and grrrreeeaat! This has been quite a surprise to my family and friends, who have known me all of my life and know that my roots are in Cambridge, Canada, not Inverness, Scotland! My accent is a consequence of the fall, and I am one of only 60 people in the world who has been diagnosed with a foreign dialect as a result of stroke or acquired brain injury.

Although my new wee brogue is an adjustment I could live with, there were many changes that have been challenging and difficult. After the fall, I soon realized that my three friends Chaos, Mayhem, and Confusion were no longer compadres. I had trouble coping with drop-off times for the children at my camps, questions from staff or parents for where the children were to go, what they were to do next, and loud noises.

I would often find myself a quiet corner away from the chaos and confusion of the camp to help cope with the post-concussion symptoms I was feeling. At noon each day I would go to the house to rest and would remain in my dark quiet bedroom as sleep would bid me a time of solace for 2-3 hours. My dark bedroom and sleep became my only escape from the chaos around me.

Everything seemed to become a haze of activity, and I cannot tell you to this day how everything necessary to run a camp, horse farm, and busy family got completed. Yet everything seemed to operate, thanks to my husband, mother-in-law, kids, and friends. I only know that I was exhausted and even sitting watching TV or hearing the pots and pans clang and utensils hit the plate irritated me and made me escape to my room time and time again.

I continued for years feeling guilty and anxious because I was not available or helpful to my family. I didn't realize until this year when I was talking to a friend at a conference that I had continued to blame and berate myself for allowing this to happen. Yet, she noted, it was an accident; it was not something I had chosen. The weight of the guilt I had carried for years seemed to be lifted in that very moment.

My friend also helped me to understand that I was grieving the loss of the woman I had been. I had been flowing through the stages of grief as Elizabeth Kubler Ross had written about in her 1969 book *On Death and Dying*. Yet it was not *someone* I had lost—it was *me* that I had lost. She had literally died, and I needed to adapt to this new individual whom I felt was incompetent, unable to cope, and experienced severe anxiety.

I wanted control over my life again. I wanted the ability to fly and soar with speed and confidence, as I had done before. I yelled at God for the injustice.

Why had this happened? How was I supposed contribute to life when I did not even know who I had become? Where was the person who so easily swept through life taking each new challenge with vigor and exhilaration?

But, my friends, just because I coped less didn't mean it was hopeless, as I would soon learn.

After struggling with my new reality for three years, I'd finally had enough, enough of feeling frustrated, enough of feeling isolated, and enough of being unable to cope with day-to-day life. So over the next few years, I researched and tested a multitude of traditional and non-traditional therapeutic coping strategies, until I devised a holistic routine that provided me with the relief I was desperately seeking.

Slowly, but surely, I emerged from my cocooned state and rejoined the world, born anew. I began to realize that there was much that I should, and could, be "grate-full" for in the midst of the tragedy of the "great fall."

Here is just a wee bit of what Malachi, whose name means "Messenger of God" has taught me.

Malachi has taught me what my priorities should be. He has taught me about what I really need, not just what I want. Our newest technologies and toys only excite us for a time. We crave more speed, noise, gadgets, brain numbing TV, or a stimulating Wii game to cover our true feelings of sadness, loneliness, and lack of true connection with others and ourselves. Thomas Merton, an American writer and mystic, states, "We are so obsessed with doing that we have no time and no imagination left for being."

Malachi's greatest message is to be still, rest, and be kind to yourself and others. As I have said, I used to always be one to get'r done! Now I can't, at least not the way I used to. However, now I'm able to live in moments, incredible moments, where I am able to be still, breathe and soak in the sunsets, full moons, deer running in our fields, and fall colors and smells.

One night when I went to fill the water tank, Malachi met me at the gate, as he usually does. He rested his head on my left shoulder, then gently, quietly, and ever so slowly, lifted his head and put it on my right shoulder. I felt him push his neck towards my ear, and I could hear his heartbeat and breathing. It felt like the very rhythm of life. To me, it was a sacred moment in time. If I had not fallen, if I had not had this accident, I would have missed the very rhythm of life. Be sure to pause in your day, and acknowledge the slightest good, positive, and hopeful part of your life. Be sure to catch one breath or hear one heart beat to feel the very presence of God.

My 15-year-old daughter, Mikayla, wrote this on her mirror, which we share as a favorite quote taken from Nicolas Spark's *The Last Song:*

> I have faith that God will show you the answer. But you have to understand that sometimes it takes a while to be able to recognize what God wants you to do. That's how it often is. God's voice is usually nothing more than a whisper, and you have to listen very carefully to hear it. But other times, in those rarest of moments, the answer is obvious and rings as loud as a church bell.

I know God has been ringing the bell strong and hard for me! It says, "Wake up and smell the coffee and the roses; embrace your children; love your husband; appreciate your friends; and spend time in my garden of green grass, towering trees, and with my precious animals. Be Still."

Be still and connect to the unwavering strength that you will find within by creating quiet moments in the midst your day. My prayer for you is that you know the sacredness of life and to be "Grate-Full" now without ever having to experience the "great fall."

About the Author

Sharon Campbell-Rayment is a motivational speaker, author, and workshop facilitator dedicated to helping people cope better with day-to-day life. She holds a Bachelor of Science degree in Nursing, a Master of Divinity degree, and is the founder of The Coping Clinic. Sharon also is a facilitator of the Labyrinth Experience and a facilitator of Equine Experiential Learning. Sharon has been interviewed for radio, print, and television in numerous countries around the world. She is also one of only 60 people worldwide diagnosed with Foreign Accent Syndrome. Visit Sharon's website www.thecopingclinic.com to learn more about her coping techniques.

Happiness is a Choice

Jennifer Colford

*"No one can grant you happiness. Happiness is a choice
we all have the power to make."*
—Dean Koontz

Though it is very difficult to seek happiness when you are in the depths of despair, it is then that you must show unwavering strength and determination to achieve your recovery. This strength and determination will reward you with the happiness you seek.

I remember the joy I felt when I thought of my beautiful little girl, who would be turning two just before our new baby would be joining our family for Christmas. We were creating our dream of a house full of children, and it was a very happy time for me.

But disaster struck in my fourth month of pregnancy.

My husband had a mental breakdown and was institutionalized. I wished, hoped, and prayed that he would get better. As days turned into weeks and weeks into months with no change in my husband's condition, I began to fear that our dream might not turn out as we had planned.

Our son's birth was a bittersweet moment for me. The doctors thought the birth of his child might help my husband, so they sedated him and off we went to the hospital.

Those glorious words, "It's a boy!" were thrilling and exciting! But they were also very sad because at that moment I knew my husband was not going to get better. Though he was there for the baby's birth, his mind was somewhere far, far away.

The months that followed were difficult as I struggled to balance being a single parent and a caregiver. Seven months after our son was born and just five weeks before our daughter's third birthday, my husband committed suicide. I was devastated.

When he died, I felt like he took all my hopes and dreams with him. I was grieving, I was angry, and I was scared.

How could I possibly raise two babies when I could hardly breathe from the crushing pain in my chest? At first, the pain was overwhelming. But as days, weeks, and months passed, the pain became slightly less unbearable.

Then I made a decision. I decided I was going to be happy again. Despite the pain that was my constant companion, I began doing things that made me happy in the days before my husband's illness.

I started taking guitar lessons. I reacquainted myself with my favorite beach, and I began to talk to friends about life in general, not about how I was doing.

My family was thrilled! When I asked my mom why she was so insistent I join my friends for our weekly fire and sing-along on the beach, she gave me a sad smile and said, "Don't you realize how long it's been since we heard you laugh? We thought we had lost you too."

How tragic it would have been if I had remained the empty shell of a human being that I was for so long—moving on autopilot, just trying to get through the moment. My beloved children would have lost both of their parents.

When I recognized this, I began to search for the blessings in my life. The more I searched, the more apparent it became that they were there all along. My children were healthy and happy, I had a loving and supportive family, and I had some really great friends. I began to enjoy and appreciate life again.

When I was drowning in despair I reached out to the Universe, and the Universe threw me a lifeline. The very moment I decided to be happy, the road to happiness appeared.

This is a lesson I hold close to my heart: You can't always choose your circumstances, but if you seek good, even in your darkest hours, you will be sure to find it.

I cannot explain why some things happen in life. I wish I had a magic wand that would wipe away the setbacks and sorrows people face. However, I do know there is always hope, and there is always good. You just need to make the decision to find it.

Life can be tough sometimes, but each obstacle you overcome makes you stronger and more alive. Always look for the good, especially in the face of adversity. Search for, find, and appreciate the good in life, and you will surely be rewarded for your effort.

Though it is very difficult to seek happiness when you are in the depths of despair, it is then that you must show unwavering strength and determination in your search. This strength and determination will reward you with the happiness you seek.

About the Author

Jennifer Colford is an International Best-Selling author with her book *Managing Mothering: Simple Shifts to Help You Become the Best Mom on the Planet*. She is a coach and mentor and her life's purpose is to live and help others live in joy and abundance. Jennifer lives in Newfoundland with her two children and their Great Dane puppy, Beaner. Learn more about Jennifer's work at http://JenniferColford.com.

Resplendent in Death: Gifts from My Mother

Corinne L. Casazza

"Your sacred heart is full of Light, and this Light will take care of you."
—Sai Maa

It hardly seems possible that my mom has been gone for five years. There are still days when I think "I have to call ma." and then remember I don't. For me, losing her was a huge lesson in being present and knowing there is joy in every moment.

When my mom, Betty, was diagnosed with uterine cancer, I had just relocated from Boston to Sedona, Arizona. In the next few years, she had two major surgeries as well as chemo and radiation.

One cold November night in 2008, Betty watched her own mother pass on. That same evening, my mother fell, breaking her ankle in two places. We'd find out later her back was also fractured. She'd never sleep lying down again, the pain in her back too great. We had no way of knowing that six months later my mother would be gone.

In April 2009, she spent ten days in the hospital. Blood clots were making treatment difficult. She needed to walk to get her blood flowing, but her broken ankle and back made movement nearly impossible. Shortly after returning home, she was rushed back to the hospital with difficulty breathing. She had a blood clot that had actually passed through her heart. The doctor was astounded. "Your mother has a very strong heart," she said. "This would've killed most people."

I was told my mother was being released from the hospital, but it didn't feel that way to me. It didn't feel as if she were coming home at all. I got on a plane. Had I not listened to my intuition and headed east right then, I wouldn't have been with her when she passed.

When I landed in Boston, my sister, Donna, told me to come directly to the hospital. Blood clots again. "Prepare yourself," Donna warned. "She's lost a lot of weight and she's frail. She doesn't look like herself. Don't be afraid."

I felt sick to my stomach and fear rising. What would she look like? How would I feel when I saw her? How would I react?

When I arrived, my mother was sitting up watching the Bruins game. She was a huge hockey and football fan. She looked small, even shriveled. Her once brilliant mane of red hair falling out. Her foot was an angry purple-black because of the clots.

She told me her foot hurt, but she was happy to see me. I surprised myself by sitting at her bedside and taking her hand. Since she didn't want to be alone, Donna and I slept by her bed at night. We watched a home shopping channel, and talked about which gemstones we liked best. My mother loved jewelry and had traveled the world buying golden stone-encrusted treasures wherever she went. "The more bling, the better the ring," we joked, pointing at the screen.

As I tried to sleep that night, fear welled up inside me. Panic. Shortness of breath. An anxiety attack. I recognized it clearly, it was like the fire-breathing dragon under my childhood bed, and it reared its ugly head every time mine hit the pillow.

I was having a tough time being present. It was a few days before my birthday. I didn't want to be in Boston on my birthday. I had plans with friends in Sedona that meant a lot to me. I knew I was being incredibly selfish and in that moment, I didn't care. I was frustrated and just wished my mother's illness would go away. Why couldn't things be the way they used to be? She could be healthy and I could be in Sedona.

The next day they told my mother there was nothing more they could do for her. Even though my intuition had told me this, the news was still shocking. I was very torn. I felt very blessed to be there with her, and also incredibly sad it really would be the end. My mother was very eloquent and emphatic telling the hospice nurses she only wanted medication to keep her comfortable, and no resuscitation. I remember feeling how brave she was, how unwavering her strength, even in the face of death. I left the room to cry. It didn't seem fair. One day she was going home and the next she was dying! Suddenly getting back to Sedona didn't seem so important.

Later that afternoon, a priest came to give her last rites. I've never been much of a Catholic, preferring spirituality to religion, but you can bet I prayed with the priest and my parents. My mother asked me to take her glasses off and I knew she'd never ask for them again.

Even after all this, I still wasn't present. I kept identifying my mother with the body in that bed, even though spiritually I knew better. I was agitated and just wished she'd stop breathing. It was so difficult to watch her deteriorate: I just wanted it to end. I wanted her suffering and fear to end. I realize how cold this sounds. I didn't judge my thoughts and feelings. I simply allowed myself to have them. I allowed them to pass through me.

I called a friend for some guidance. "What is the one thing that needs healing in your relationship with your mother?" she asked.

My answer was immediate, "She could never see who I am."

My friend said, "Her heart is so strong because she has so much unconditional love for you all. She's more in spirit than in body now and every time her heart beats, it's a gift for you from the other side. She's sending you love from the other side."

I felt the truth of this as the hair on my arms stood on end. My friend said that all my mother could see was the love and light that I am. The love and light of all of us. She was just watching us in wonder and wasn't quite ready to go yet.

These words comforted me. I returned to my mother's bedside and held her hand, but I still wasn't present. As I sat with her, my eyes grew wide in recognition. I got it. I understood the source of my anxiety attacks. I was afraid if my mother died without seeing who I am, I'd never know myself.

This realization shifted something. Relief flooded my body. I knew this was an opportunity to see and feel more deeply into who I am. My friend's words had comforted me, and now I was buoyed. My mother was more in spirit than in body and this was something to celebrate. I knew she was not the form lying in that bed. I understood what she is, what we all are, can never die. I began breathing through my heart and crying tears of joy. I was finally present!

As I relaxed, I could feel my mother all around me. She was half in and half out of her body. Her spirit filled the room; the energy was jubilant. She was crossing over. I was resplendent in this truth and just sat with her in the energy.

At some point I realized that the energy had been there all along and I was just too wrapped up in my own story to notice. That was my choice in the moment. And so what? I'm present now!

My mother's passing made me more aware that there is joy in every moment, and when we're not wrapped up in our agenda, we are free to enjoy it. Further, even though something may not look like a gift in the moment, it is! The universe is always conspiring to bring us to our highest good. When we pay attention and are free of story and present, we can feel it. My mother left me this great gift as her legacy to me.

About the Author

Corinne L. Casazza is an author and energy worker in Boston, Massachusetts. Whether she's writing, teaching or facilitating a healing session, Corinne's intention is to help others find their joy and passion in daily life. Corinne has published two novels, many magazine articles and a myriad of marketing pieces. Her second novel Walk Like an Egyptian is available online. She's currently at work on her third. Corinne has had the good fortune to interview many of the top names in personal growth including Joan Borysenko, Caroline Myss, Jean Houston, Dr. Joe Dispenza, Judith Orloff and the late Sylvia Browne. Corinne feels strongly that creativity and humor allow us to find our own inner light. For more information, visit her web site at CorinneCasazza.com or her Amazon author page at: www.amazon.com/author/corinnecasazza.

Deep Purple

Rebecca Field

"Someday, after mastering the winds, waves, the tides, and gravity, we shall harness for God the energies of love, and then, for a second time in the history of the world, man will have discovered fire."
—Pierre Teilhard de Chardin

Disconsolate and numb, I walked out of the doctor's office with eyes cast downward, still hearing the icy medical voice with her seemingly triumphant pronouncement that I had epilepsy.

So this is what it was! I was an epileptic with what seemed like no possibility of ever living a normal life, There were no tears, only the feeling that somehow I had to get through this. But how could I with the drug the doctor had prescribed?

The drug made me sleepy and depressed. It left me unable to think or feel much of anything. I was in deep purple, unending deep purple. I wondered if I'd always be in this dark and horrific place. After all, if I were like this all my life, I wouldn't be able to do much for anybody or even for myself.

I was nineteen, and my whole future was before me. Yet there was no future, no way I'd ever be able to do the things I had dreamed about doing. My heart yearned to go to the far ends of the earth: to Russia, Japan, India and working for a higher education.

I managed to get back to the university dorm, where I slept until the next morning. When I awakened I found my roommate was getting ready for her first class. I scrambled to get to my first class too, a class on writing skills. That day the professor passed out a yellow number 2 pencil with an eraser to everyone in the class. Each pencil was identical, new, like all the others. The assignment was to write a five-hundred-word essay and describe the pencil in minute detail without using any words that had feeling content. I had enormous trouble with the assignment.

At that time writing an essay was an almost insurmountable task because I couldn't write in sentences any longer than three or four words. Likewise when I spoke, a three or four word sentence was all I could utter. Because of the prescribed medicine, I was barely capable of functioning with any intelligence at all. Life as a university student became impossible. My grades plummeted, and I finally flunked out.

I recall going to a movie with some chums one evening. As we exited the theater, I felt the desperation of total loneliness. The deep purple loneliness without recourse to any human relationships for a lifetime engulfed me. I felt like a leper...unwanted, unneeded, and unwelcome.

My parents saw that I was in real trouble and contacted a friend about helping me. They seemed to have intuitively known that an unconventional method of healing and educating would work with me. The collaborator they chose was a highly unusual woman, largely self-educated, and a seamstress by trade. She also wrote Shakespearean-style sonnets with perfect rhyme and meter for the Bard's time and style.

They arranged for me to go to Margo's apartment that very Saturday afternoon. Fortunately she knew me before the drugs had taken over, in that time seemingly long ago when the sun shone on my life and there was joy and promise. Now I was in deep purple and neither hope nor possibility was anywhere on the horizon.

Margo always lovingly took me in, and our two hour sessions flew by as she showed me some of the notebooks she had filled with drawings that explained concepts so advanced for me that I could not begin to understand them. Occasionally she would read me one or two of her Shakespearean sonnets. Even though I was too sick to grasp what they meant, somewhere in my being there were the fluttering wings of a thousand enchanted butterflies promising unwavering strength through my work with her. Margo worked with me on developing self-esteem. She helped me drop an attitude of victimization and instead to recognize and use positive qualities.

Week after week we worked together. Sometimes she taught me how to work with affirmations to heal myself with a more optimistic outlook. Other times she took a more professorial approach and taught me many things, especially about human relationships. We told stories, and I related incidents that stood out during the week.

I was working on trying to understand why my parents were in such opposition. Why was there such a huge divergence in their belief systems? Why did they each feel their way of seeing the world was right? Which one was right? Finding the "right answer" plagued me. Then on one of my visits Margo simply told me each was right for himself or herself.

Somehow that did nothing for me, and I couldn't understand it. My cotton-like cocoon was still deep purple. As I knew the world at that time, there was a definite beginning and end point to life. After all there is birth and death!

On one of my more dense days with Margo, she walked me to the elevator as I left. She shocked me when she grasped me by the shoulders, looked me in the eyes with memorable kindness and powerful intensity and said, "If there is one thing I can tell you, it is that consciousness is everything."

I managed to dredge up all I could find in me to say, "Yes, I know."

But in my heart at that time, I didn't really feel like I knew much of anything. Yet, I have always remembered what she said.

The most significant thing Margo did for me was take me off drugs. Over a period of about two years, this marvelous and compassionate woman who had not gone beyond the eighth grade did the impossible. She monitored me carefully over the next two years, and as I decreased the dosage of the medicine my sight started to come back.

She counseled me to walk a lot and to swim several times a week. As I did, I lost weight, and my vision became sharper. I was even able to speak well-formulated adult sentences. Over the time that the drug left my system, I began to make friends again. I could think with reasonable clarity. The great gift was to see again. Depression no longer hovered over me.

I was free!

My life had direction and purpose. I had moved from the deep purple phase of my life to one of unwavering strength. I continued to use the ideas that Margo had so patiently and lovingly taught me. With her help and my own strong determination, I managed to complete my undergraduate work and went on to get a master's and a doctorate degree.

Out of my studies, travels, and life experience, I eventually wrote a book entitled, *To Choose the Fire of the Cosmos,* which is an explanation of Gandhi's statement, "We [individual and collective humanity] are the ones we have been waiting for."

I married a wonderful man who changed the face of the earth with his computer programs. I have been around the world twice, once on a yearlong trip by myself, and the second time with my adult son. We have two sons, whose love and respect for their father are touching. We adopted a beautiful Tibetan refugee daughter, who now lives and works near San Francisco.

I have seen and experienced the beauties of Japan, felt the warmth, magic, and joy of living of the Russians, and the stately wisdom of India, and I can say that humanity is sound. Through ourselves and our qualities, we bring great hope about the future.

I started an international educational nonprofit organization and worked for fifteen years with Tibetan refugees in India and poor women in Russia and Ukraine. These women became successful entrepreneurs using the Russian business style.

Service became my calling, and through my small nonprofit organization and the help of a magnificent and inspired Russian colleague, together we reached over 50,000 people in the Saratov area. We provided them with practical entrepreneurial training and health education that enabled them to care for their own health problems, like heart disease and diabetes. We also taught young girls and boys how to avoid the cruel entrapment of sex slavery.

Now, nearly an octogenarian, I am developing a group across the United States who work to end mass imprisonment of people of color. My online business, teaching and writing about the importance of service to others keeps me active. I am also on a volunteer committee with the United Nations and have met brilliant, deeply caring people from all over the world who work quietly in the background of the ubiquitous maelstroms that face us all. We work together to create a living and life-honoring process of developing unwavering strength for ourselves and humanity, our beautiful planet, and the other kingdoms of nature.

About the Author

Service became my calling, and through my small nonprofit organization and the help of a magnificent and inspired Russian colleague, together we reached over 50,000 people in the Saratov area. We also taught young girls and boys how to avoid the cruel entrapment of sex slavery. Now, nearly an octogenarian, I am developing a group across the United States who work to end mass imprisonment of people of color. My online business, teaching and writing about the importance of service to others keeps me active. I am also on a volunteer committee with the United. Out of my studies, travels and life experience, I eventually wrote a book called *To Choose the Fire of the Cosmos*.

Faith Happened

Deb Scott

"God is more anxious to bestow His blessings on us than we are to receive them. For it is not God's way that great blessings should descend without the sacrifice first of great sufferings."
—Saint Augustine of Hippo

I certainly didn't feel blessed. I was in survival mode. Everything hurt in my heart, mind, body, and soul. I was exhausted and numb from so much pain. I felt like I was dying along with the parents for whom I had become the sole caregiver.

From the outside, my life appeared to be going along rather well. I had a few skeletons in the closet like everyone else, but I never felt my lot in life was any worse than anyone else I had met.

I had earned my biology degree and turned it into a very successful cardiac surgery sales career for twenty years. I made a good six figure paycheck, had a chance to get married a couple of times, traveled, built a house, and I had shelves filled with trophies and awards to validate my worldly success.

So what happened? I will tell you what happened. Life happened. Death happened. Financial devastation happened. Faith happened.

The illusion of what I thought was a good life full of meaning died with two major life events: my parents passed away and a million dollars was stolen from me in a banking Ponzi scheme shortly after they passed. Family left, friends disappeared and fear became a shadow I couldn't kill. Who was I, and what was I doing here in this skin suit?

My mom had become my best friend in the last ten years of her life. As an only child, I couldn't truly understand the value of that rare gift until she was gone.

The days of driving her to Massachusetts General Hospital for her chemotherapy and radiation treatments became complete journeys in them-

144

selves. We talked, we prayed, and we forgave. We discovered each other in ways that could never have happened had it not been for the cancer, and in that process, the most amazing discovery was that of ourselves.

I remember wandering the halls of Mass General alone early one morning, when everything had changed. Just a few months earlier, I had been rockin' my power suit, visiting surgeons for discussions about products and observing someone else's mother, father, brother, or sister in surgery. I was in control. Then suddenly, I was just a child-like daughter, with two parents having surgery the same day at different ends of the hospital. I visited each one in their respective recovery rooms, and each one asked me about the condition of the other. I will never forget that day.

I don't know exactly when the things I hated about the past unexpectedly became the seeds of today's blessings, but I am here to tell you they did, and they are. People don't change because they see the light; they change because they feel the heat.

We were driving back home from mom's treatment in Boston one afternoon, going over the Tobin Bridge when the words ran right out of my mouth before I could think to catch them. "When you die mom, I'm going to lose my best friend. I don't know what I'm going to do without you."

She was so quick and confident in her response I thought she must have heard my thoughts before I did. "Deborah, God will always send someone into your life to take care of you."

And while I could write hundreds of pages filled with all the sad stories of despair, betrayal, and injustice in my life, my story is about unwavering strength and how each of us can really find it in a tangible way.

What is the secret ingredient to transforming the events and emotions you hate about your life into the very same things you treasure and appreciate most? How do you take the destruction of despair and begin to build a better life, become a better person, and actually feel grateful for those disasters?

I think the key is simply this: a humble acceptance that God exists.

I'm not talking about a Pollyanna Holy Roller type of belief in God. I am talking about digging deep into your own personal attachments in life and facing fear straight in the face. It's about leaning into your most repulsive feelings of pain, suffering, and inevitable mortality you want to avoid and pretend will never happen. Sitting in silence with your own demons takes real courage.

I have learned:
1. No one is immune to sorrow or suffering in life. It's part of our condition in the skin suit. No one else has the answer.

2. God always loves you through everything, even if you don't recognize or believe he does. Ask him for help.
3. You don't have to understand how God is helping you for God to be helping you. Trust and keep the faith.
4. Possessions will never bring you joy; only people can help you do that. Prioritize your life accordingly.
5. Reflecting often on your inevitable death will help you live a life that really matters.

I discovered most of my suffering comes from secretly wanting control, control over a person, situation, or result I have decided to expect. I want things my way, and when they don't go my way, I inevitably get a tsunami of negative emotions as a result.

I don't want my mom to die of cancer now, I don't want to take care of my dad and bury him a year after my mom. I don't want to lose a million hard-earned dollars to a banking Ponzi scheme. I don't want this to be happening the way it is happening to me!

Acceptance of what is, exactly as it is, and the inner search for how it is helping me to become a better person is the only source of strength I seek. Where is the gift for me? It is the only way I have found to make peace with my past, live in the spirit of life, give gratitude for this moment, and believe I am already in God's tender loving care for anything that will happen in my tomorrow.

Today, I pray differently from the way I did even a year ago. I'm growing. I'm not finished yet. No one is.

I pray for the grace to learn what God wants to teach me through this person or situation instead of asking for a specific result. I pray to stop thinking about myself and focus on the needs of others who are less fortunate than I. I pray to appreciate the many gifts I take for granted on a daily basis, and I pray for people who are going to die today. I pray to learn how to love God, how to love myself, and how to love everyone I meet. I pray that people are better off for having met me. I pray for people to go to heaven and experience eternal joy and peace.

About the Author

Deb Scott, BA, CPC is a four-time award winning author of *The Sky is Green and The Grass is Blue*. She also won the Best Podcaster Award for *The Best People We Know Show*, which has over 1 million global listeners and can be heard on Blog Talk Radio, Stitcher and Player FM. Having spent twenty years as a cardiovascular surgical specialist and winning numerous awards for outstanding sales and leadership skills, Deb overcame sexual abuse, others' alcoholism, dysfunctional relationships, depression and financial devastation. Today, Deb helps clients turn things around in their businesses (or in the business of living) through the discovery of their amazing selves. Sign up for Deb's free "Monthly Mind Vitamin" newsletter at http://www.GreenSkyandBlueGrass.com

My Little Switchblade

Ron McElroy

"We rejoice in our sufferings, knowing that suffering produces endurance, and endurance produces character, and character produces hope."
—Romans 5:3-4

Have you ever walked away unscathed from an erupting volcano? No? Have you been clubbed in the head with a hatchet or stabbed through the heart? On second thought, you probably wouldn't live to tell about it, so don't answer that. These extremely rare and violent experiences are things I'm confident I have felt, but in my case, I can live to tell you about it. While I cannot say I know what it feels like to die, I know very well how painful it can be to live through death. But perseverance creates greatness of character, and that is the man I choose to live as and to tell my story.

Terror grips my chest so tight it's difficult to breathe. Choked back tears burn my eyes like acid rain. I hide from the outside world, which is just darkness and garbled shouts buried in my raggedy and comfortably worn out bed covers. Acting as a protective shield, the blanket only hides the chance I might witness the growing intensity, the rumble of an erupting volcano, which is coming from just beyond my thin, closed bedroom door. Walls cannot conceal a family's every word. This time, again, it is my parents, my protectors and my caretakers, who have chosen not to care on this night—again. The lava spews just feet away.

Pulling even tighter into a fetal position and trying not to breathe through alternating sobs, screams, silence, and shoving, the blanket becomes a shield of invisibility. Short pauses are a false reprieve, but the silence only lasts for the seconds it takes to reload the verbal machine guns. The damage of this warfare is explosive, crashing and landing, crash landing. There is no air raid warning for this attack, but I am taking care and in a shelter—the shelter of my blanket, my coat of invisibility. I am not unarmed, my white knuckles gripping a small switchblade for protection, of course.

The cold point of the blade is pressed to the skin of my stomach just above my naval, resisting, holding back and holding on. Each night, like this one, I try to convince myself to push my little black switchblade deeper, harder. Thankfully, courage retreats each night behind sleep and deep exhausted dreams. On these mornings, when I try to greet the new day, my little switchblade lies next to me, reminding me of my weaknesses. But I get dressed, get my lunch and head off to school after having been emotionally stabbed in the heart. Yet, I lived to tell the tale.

Growing up we try to please others; it feels good. I was a typical all-star athlete, which pleased many people: my family, my coaches, peers and community. While my physical strength and successes grew in sports, so did the occurrence of frequent, head-splitting migraines. Everyone had their own theories and opinionated ideas about the cause of my migraines. Yet regardless of the treatment, they persisted and even prevented me from playing in a critical baseball game.

I had traveled miles, and people were relying upon me! What a pussy!

My dad would always make it to my games. He would watch through unfocused eyes and yell with bourbon breath. His inebriated support was one thing I could rely upon, embarrassing beyond description. My college baseball aspirations disintegrated to ashes from these debilitating migraines. I quit playing all sports. I was not swayed to reconsider, despite strong opposition and opportunities for baseball scholarships.

Now I believe I found a way to persevere, to protect myself and move forward on another path. The migraines dissipated as I got older, and they were never officially attributed to one cause. I see clearly now that they were a physical salvation. Maybe the migraines were a psychological survival mechanism. I know that pain can be a double-edged sword. I know what it feels like to have your head split with a hatchet, but I lived to tell about it.

They say that time cures all, a favorite quote I must admit. This includes physical and emotional wounds, scars included. Of course the time it takes seems eternal. Yet, come hell or high water, at some point in your lifetime, a cure for what ails you will show itself and ask you to rise to the occasion, exercise persistence, find stamina, and use strength. It is up to you to see it, to recognize it, to acknowledge it, act upon it, use your strength and "deal," as they say. It is up to you alone to look for it, to want it and to actively seek it out. This is the power of choice you have in your life.

What a shame to not be able to exercise the power of choice in life. If you're dealt a bad hand, such as being born into hopeless poverty, into insidious dysfunctional wealth, or with a terminal or incurable disease, you have the strength to choose the way you want to live your life.

Every one of us can remember a friend or an acquaintance who overcame extreme adversity. Or maybe you simply read a story about a person overcoming incredible obstacles. They had all the odds stacked against them, yet they persevered and lived to tell their story. Most of the time you learn they are gracious with less and magnificent, even though they may come from nothing. These heroes move mountains.

"The man who moves a mountain begins by carrying small stones."
—Confucius

When the obstacles are great, it is a sign to get to work. The word persevere contains the word "severe" for a reason. Severe obstacles make for the greatest accomplishments. Besides knowing what you want, you have to want it more than you want to breathe.

The voices in our head try to snuff your inner fire, the volcanic, explosive energy of life that is in you. You can hear the voices complaining, leading you off the path to an easier or more comfortable trail. It gives you permission to repeat, "Woe is me!"

You complain, play the victim and justify, all the while going nowhere, walking in place. Your inner voice may be muffled under blankets, hidden behind pain or sobs, but if you listen, you will hear its challenge. Your true inner voice, not the voices of others, will always dare you to persevere, summon your courage to face the mountain, and give you the character and strength to live to tell your story of triumph.

About the Author

The author Ron McElroy is the founder and CEO of ROC (Real Office Centers) which offers commercial office space in prestigious markets across Southern California which cater to entrepreneurs in an array of prominent industries. Around the office he is the "Big Kahuna" and not just for his true Hawaiian characteristic manner, but sheer respect emanates from his peers for his large and generous ideals, for the endless support he displays to his friends and colleagues, along with philanthropic endeavors and expanding locations, the nickname is deserved. McElroy had the inspiration of reflection and time to undertake writing his best-selling touching memoir entitled *Wrong Side of the Tracks* only to discover that there was more to his story and that his true happiness is derived from creating, growing, nurturing and participating in the success of others.

Water, Water Everywhere

Bill King

"You can conquer almost any fear if you will only make up your mind to do so. For remember, fear doesn't exist anywhere except in the mind."
—Dale Carnegie

When I was only eight years old, I nearly drowned.

As you can imagine, I developed a healthy fear of open water after that!

Twenty years later, that fear was still controlling my life, but my plan was easy: avoidance. Choices I made kept me from having to face them.

Then it happened.

My wife gave me a cruise for our 10th anniversary.

I got her a beautiful diamond ring, yet she gave me a gift of death! Her rationale was solid. She had researched and found the shortest cruise possible. Her belief was that if the cruise was short enough, I would be able to overcome my fear. She had found the perfect death sentence: a trip from Fort Lauderdale to the Bahamas. "You can do it, honey! It's only six hours!"

Her eyes were filled with hope and excitement, but all I heard was an eerie tune from my childhood. "Just sit right back and you'll hear a tale, a tale of a fateful trip . . . a six hour tour, a six hour tour."

I KNEW I shouldn't get on that boat! There were so many omens it was as if I were one of those people in a horror movie when they hear voices whispering, "Get out!"

Omen #1, it was raining when we woke up.

152

Omen #2, easels stood at every doorway proclaiming, "Warning, rough seas. Take necessary precautions."

Murderously, my wife pushed me past each one toward the biggest breakfast buffet on the planet, where I ate like I was not going to eat for the next three days: omen #3.

Then I realized that I never took any Dramamine: omen #4.

The staff lined seasick bags along all the rails: omen #5.

Then a big gust of wind came and didn't subside: omen #6.

With fear of the ocean sitting squarely on my shoulders, our boat headed off to my fateful, calculated death.

Water, water everywhere, and the last thing I wanted was a drink.

Once we were undocked, we moved slowly out of the port and into the Gulf Stream.

The first hour on death row was not too bad. My delusional mind thought that it would be over quickly since it was only a six hour tour . . . a six hour tour. In the third hour, we encountered higher and higher seas. Ten-foot seas became fifteen-foot seas, which quickly gave way to twenty-foot seas. A friendly tugboat captain was kind enough to educate us. He exclaimed, "I'm on these waters every day, son, and that right there is a twenty-five foot wave!"

My stomach fluttered into my throat as the sea became rougher and rougher. We were tossed back and forth so badly I decided I would go inside. As I walked in, I nearly passed out. Remember omen #3, the breakfast? Well, it seemed everyone in that room remembered it too because it was everywhere. The smell was so obnoxious I quickly went back outside.

I was so terrified I started thinking in segments. If we could just stay afloat for six more thirty-minute segments, we might survive. Feeling quite relieved that I had this thing figured out, I began counting minutes.

Then suddenly and without warning, my chair catapulted across the deck toward the water. I was hurdling to my death as I watched my life flash before my eyes.

My chair hit the railing, and I gasped for breath. I was nearly thrown off the boat! I kid you not! My wife tried to reassure me, "Honey, it's going to be alright. We only have two hours left."

Completely rattled, I dragged the heavy chair back to its original spot. Now I had a new plan: stand with my arms and legs wrapped around a mounted pole for the next two hours.

As the boat rocked, nausea began to rise to serious levels. In the movies, you see people get sick in public all the time, but when it happens for real it's a whole different story. Finally omen #3 emerged. Embarrassed, humiliated, with tears in my eyes, I glared at the spectators like Maximus in *Gladiator*.

ARE YOU NOT ENTERTAINED?

Water, water everywhere, and the last thing I wanted was a drink.

Then I saw it! LAND! My heart leapt, and hope returned! Thank you, God, thank you! I enthusiastically told my wife that I would pay $10,000 to take a flight back to Florida. There was no way I was getting back on that boat! I watched with hysterical glee as we drew nearer to solid ground.

All of a sudden one of the ship's bartenders waved his arms shouting, "THERE'S THE PORT! I'VE BEEN DOING THIS FIVE YEARS, AND I KNOW THAT'S THE PORT! I SEE IT EVERYDAY, AND WE JUST PASSED IT!"

No, I thought as some kind of vice gripped my heart, no way! He's got to be mistaken! My lungs heaved as I soberly watched the island go by.

A few minutes later the speakers blasted, "We have been advised that the seas are too rough for us to enter the port. For the safety of the passengers, we have been advised to turn back."

Turn back? Safety of the passengers? It was a good thing the captain was nowhere in sight, because I am certain his safety was in jeopardy!

My hope for life vanished. We were dead. I lost all hope and began to wonder who would take care of our son back home.

Water, water everywhere, and the last thing I wanted was a drink.

The waves grew from 25 feet to 35 feet to 45 feet to 55 feet! Front, back, left, right. Front, back, left, right. This had been going on for about 7 1/2 hours now, but the latest waves started rocking us like this: Front, back, left, hold, left some more, bottles crashing, then right, hold, a little farther right, more right, bottles crashing, things breaking.

After over eight hours, avoiding the restroom was no longer an option. I had a mission: in and out in two minutes.

The restroom was tiny, and the ship was swaying back and forth so badly I couldn't even stand up. My head hit all four walls, but I was determined to be a man and stand up. After five minutes I gave up. I have never before in my life had to sit down; it was humiliating. My dignity gone, I made my way back to the deck noticing the other men's defeated expressions. I knew we shared an unspoken bond that night.

No longer safe to stay outside on the deck, we were forced inside. As we sat on the floor, I peered out the foggy windows. Several times all I could see was water crashing over the deck on both sides. Yes, on both sides! I choked back a sob, wishing it would all just end.

Water, water everywhere, and the last thing I wanted was a drink.

The rocking left and right started to last longer and longer on each side. All kidding aside, we were seriously going down. To make matters even worse, there were some Spanish-speaking crewmembers screaming at each other while dropping things off the sides of the boat. They yelled at each other with horror in their eyes. Now, I don't speak Spanish, but I can definitely understand "panic-ese"!

I thought about what my last words were going to be, but all I could think of were swear words! Yes, friends, my final words were going to be curse words. I was doomed for all of eternity. It is the hell express for me with my very own toll tag. You are supposed to enter the afterlife on a good note, not cussing profusely. So to save my soul, I said nothing else aloud for the remainder of the trip. I held on to a support pole with one arm and seized my wife's hand with my other hand.

Water, water everywhere, and the last thing I wanted was a drink.

Finally too frightened to even open my eyes, I started praying. But I was so scared I couldn't finish. Then, I understood for the first time why I was forced to memorize prayers as a child. I focused my thoughts on those prayers as I repeated them over and over like a mantra. Slowly I retreated inward. As I went deeper and deeper, the screaming and crying all around me faded away. I believe this is how I survived. When I retreated and let go of the catastrophe around me, these prayers gave me unwavering strength to survive.

The rocking finally subsided, and someone across the boat shouted that they saw city lights ahead. I lifted my head, and my eyes met my wife's. Her reassuring smile said it all: WE WERE ALIVE! WE HAD MADE IT! We stood up, held each other and cried.

The trauma we all experienced on that trip was completely surreal. Hearing everyone crying, screaming, and knowing that any moment we could be in the water drowning almost felt like we had been to war. Several people were taken to the hospital before we could disembark, and we found out one poor man had died of a heart attack.

Later we learned we had experienced the earliest tropical storm on record in that region. The seas got as high as 65 feet, and the winds were sustained at 70 MPH with wind gusts much higher. If we had taken our trip the day before or after, we would have missed it. I am neither a statistician nor a gambler, but try to calculate the odds of me being on that boat, at that time, on that day, and the freak tropical storm flaring up over our exact location. There was a reason I was on that boat.

As I look back now, I am truly grateful. I believe that the boat made me face my deepest fear. If I could make it through that, I could make it through anything. With my fear in check, over the course of the next several months I landed a great job in a big city, got a huge promotion, and started my own side business.

In the years that followed I learned I could process my feelings and overcome my fears using humor. Later, I took it a step further and started using humor to help kids overcome the obstacles they are faced with.

Today I am excited about the uncertainties that lie ahead! And though I may feel fear from time-to-time, I now see it as a sign to change my thinking. When fear appears, I smash it down with, "Not today, buddy! Not today!" I then practice positive thinking with visualization to eliminate the fear altogether. I will never again let fear cripple me and make my choices for me!

Water, water everywhere, and I think I'll have a drink!

About the Author

Bill King is a writer, speaker, and mentor. A master of designing and implementing processes to simplify complex issues with amazing results, he used this gift to design fun, exciting and educational ideas to help kids deal with negativity, low self-esteem, bullying and anger. In addition, Bill is a certified DDI, Inc. (Developmental Dimensions International) trainer and has conducted hundreds of training classes, seminars, and workshops. His life's mission is to provide service to others to help them define and achieve their goals. Bill has written several books, notably *7 Days to Inner Peace: The Building Blocks of Awareness,* and the adolescent's version called *The Building Blocks of Creation: An Adolescent's Guide to Awareness.* http://www.idontstink.com/

Enduring Strength

Brian Glidden

"Strength does not come from physical capacity. It comes from an indomitable will."
—Mahatma Gandhi

There is something about the smell of rain on the hot summer sidewalk in Brooklyn. It represents the perfect marriage of man and nature. To me it feels like God is trying to wash away all the pain we inflict on each other, but really it's just rain on the sidewalk.

I can feel the burn as the booze makes it way down my throat, and I know relief is on the way. All painful moments of my life will be gone in a matter of minutes. Everyone leaves, and all that is left is me, God, and the earth beneath my feet . . . and the smell of the rain.

I can't remember much before I was eight. I only have snapshots of my life before the morning in 1968 when everything changed. That Saturday is like a movie in my mind. I was starting my first job. Mom made me breakfast and served me coffee that was mostly milk and sugar. I felt like the man of the house. The sun was very bright, and the air was just cool enough to see my breath. I remember walking the two blocks to my favorite candy store just above the Winthrop Street entrance of the #3 train. I made that same walk every day until I was twelve, passing the store and the men who ran it. I looked in every time, searching for the pieces of my soul left on the bathroom floor.

One of the brothers called me into the store so I could start to work. I straightened out comic books and candy bars. I felt so big, so proud of who I had become. I didn't know or understand what would come. I didn't know that who I was would disappear that day, but it did. I can't tell you the size of the room or the time of day. I don't have faces in my head, but I remember smells and feelings.

The sun was gone. The world of comic books and games and laughter had left me. I was a vessel, empty and used up. That day defined me and the direction my life would take, but it did not define my destination. I got up, pulled up my pants, and owned it all.

I started telling you about my journey when I was eight. I wasn't born at eight; I was just tempered by trauma at that age. I come from a broken family, and I've had some issues.

I was born in Brooklyn in 1960. My mother and father divorced when I was just two years old. My brother Jeff was two years older, and he was more affected by my father leaving. I don't think that wound ever healed for him. We lived in a small garden apartment on Brooklyn Avenue.

I think I was aware of God even when I was really young. We weren't religious, and I picked up more about religion from my friends than I did from my own home. My father was busy with a new family and never spent time with Jeff or me. Jeff became the father I never had, and I wish I could go back just to hug him. He was a bookworm and great student. He could do anything he set his mind to. I remember when he was 17, he was burning incense and chanting in his room. I thought he had lost it! Little did I know he was on the right path and I was not.

I look back at my life with mom and Jeff, and I know the decisions we made individually and as a family have altered the direction of my life. The outcome was transformational and moved me from one end state to another. I believe that is my purpose; to transform and talk about it.

What was my transformation? Fast-forward to May 17th 1987. I was a full blown alcoholic and drug addict. I avoided any human contact except when it served my addiction. Everyone had disowned me. I wasn't really in a relationship with Michelle anymore, but in my mind she was still with me. I had become a horrible man. I tormented her, and on that beautiful spring Sunday afternoon I decided I would drive over to her apartment to kill her and then kill myself. It wasn't a fleeting thought; it was a plan. That was my best thinking at the time.

I thank God that He had other plans. In a moment of clarity I reached out to someone from AA. I told him what I had planned. For the first time in a very long time, maybe even my life, I saw my behavior through somebody else's eyes. In what was my first spiritual awakening, I threw my face into my hands, burst into tears, and said "God I don't want to live this way anymore. Please help me, I can't live this way anymore."

In that moment the obsession for drugs, alcohol, and self-destruction was lifted from me. Since that moment I have not had a single addictive substance course through the veins of my body. I have been relieved from the bondage of self, and I believe it will never return.

That was my awakening, but where is my strength? What is it that makes a moment like that become a change that can endure anything? I believe God provides us with experiences that temper us. Tragedy is like the heat of a forge. When we are red hot and at the point of melting down, God plunges us into the cool waters of His Grace, and we are tempered and changed for a lifetime.

The following October on a gloomy afternoon there was a nip in the air and a sense that winter was coming. Emotions filled Jeff's brownstone like the smell of a Christmas tree when you first bring it into the house. We were resting on his bed. He weighed 90 or so pounds. AIDS had ravaged his body and stripped away any of the dignities we take for granted as healthy human beings. What wasn't stripped away was his spirit, his soul. Here he was in the last few days of his life, and he was worried about me, comforting me. I was newly sober and he was telling me that I would be ok and how to walk through his death. The last words Jeff spoke to me were, "You're stronger than you know."

Jeff wasn't the first person I knew who had died, but he was my brother and our love was deep. Today I see and understand more about Jeff's purpose then I ever have. He was the pioneer for both our lives. He had a quiet way of making it through things. That was his gift.

Jeff loved very deeply and he left a wake of joy wherever he went. I'm not sure what experiences drove him to do the things that ultimately took his life, but I'm sure they were painful. I've had those moments. Jeff's deepest wound I suspect was the loss of our father. Our dad didn't just walk away, he ran. He broke all physical communication with us. Jeff went into his wound and it defined him. It drove him into years of addiction and choices that ultimately infected his body with the disease that took his life. Those choices were his coping mechanism. But he was only 20 when he faced those fears and got sober.

Jeff never told me if his spiritual awakening came in a flash or if it came slowly. I do know I watched him for the last nine years of his life make choices that drew people in. He became a magnet of love. You couldn't help but want to be around him. It was as if he suddenly got the blueprint for his life and his purpose on earth. Jeff never wrote a book or a play or became famous, but he loved. His sobriety and the way he lived brought me from the brink of death into a life second to none! He is one of my guides and guards me and the people I love with a vengeance.

When I left Jeff's house that Sunday, the gloom turned to rain. I walked from Jeff's house down the hill in Park Slope and sought refuge in a doorway from a torrential downpour. God chose well that day. The doorway was the maternity entrance to the local hospital. New life walked past me at a furious pace. I could see almost the same range of emotions engulfing me in the faces of new and expecting parents walking by. That is the lesson Jeff was trying to share with me. Life is not a straight line; it's a circle. Change is our constant, and the pain we feel comes from resisting the change. Jeff was right; I was so much stronger than I knew.

He died three days later at age 29. Mom had wanted Jeff to live until he was 30. I found her in her bed just three days after Jeff's 30th birthday. She had died in her sleep of a broken heart.

The forging oven was on full blast, and I was at my melting point. What I found in that day was strength. It wasn't your average everyday strength. I found enduring strength. Tempered by the heat of loss and cooled by the waters of the grace of God, I found the ability to walk through anything and find the greatest good.

It was 2 a.m. the night after I buried my mother, and I sat at the dining room table I grew up at. The house was still, my family was gone and only I remained. In my deepest sorrow I spoke these words, "God, please don't make this have happened for no reason at all."

God heard my prayer, and I was changed forever.

What defines me? My unwavering strength is a strength that allows me to do more than just endure. My strength lets me see past this moment and realize God has a plan, and I am in it. Death, sickness, loss of love or money can come find me, and so can joy, love and laughter.

I always felt that God brought the rain to wash away the pain from my life. Without that cleansing I had no place in God's world. But today I know I am a child of the universe and perfect as I am. I deserve love. I deserve divine intervention, transformation, and peace.

That is what I have stumbled upon as I traveled along this path of finding myself. God is with me, in me, and of me. And if that is true, I deserve all that this universe has to offer.

There have been so many stops along the way: deaths, births, love, violence, hate and loss of self. My most important stop was the awakening that self cannot be lost, only misplaced.

So, this is your story. This is my journey, but your story. God brought us together so you could walk this path with me and He may heal you.

Stop trying to walk between the raindrops. Don't deny yourself another moment of joy. Speak a simple prayer, and then stand up and take that next step! Help another and understand life is not a dress rehearsal.

About the Author

Brian Glidden is a nationally renowned business executive, lecturer, and intuitive healer. He has spent the last several years using his abilities to help individuals suffering from addiction, illness, and the bereaved who are trying to understand the meaning behind their loss. Brian resides in a small town south of Boston, Massachusetts by the North Shore of Long Island with his children and fiancé Janice. For further information about Brian, his appearance calendar, or to subscribe to his free email newsletter, visit http://www.bglidden.com or join Brian Glidden—Enduring Strength on Facebook. Brian's mission is to help heal those touched by personal tragedy or the loss of a loved one. *Enduring Strength* is the title of his first book coming out in the spring of 2014.

You are Never Alone

Sandy Alemian

"Sometimes, the most important pieces of your life's puzzle come to you at the end of a long haul. In your brokenness we can find something that could never be broken . . . a connection to your soul, to God, and to the Other Side."
—Sandy Alemian

I imagine I must have had a conversation with God before I was born: "Sandy, here's what your life will be like: You'll give birth to a beautiful daughter, then you'll have two miscarriages, then you'll have a second little angel, but she will die after 31 days, and then exactly one year and one day later, you'll give birth to a healthy beautiful son. Six years later, you'll go through a divorce, then a bankruptcy. But, in the midst of it, you'll find a source of wisdom and strength to help you. You'll write about it, you'll speak about it, you'll be a source of strength to so many people, and you'll tap into a source of peace that few will ever experience. Deal . . . or no deal?"

I don't remember answering, "Deal."

I am exhausted. I am torn. I miss Ariana (she's two and a half) She is staying with my parents. Rich is having a really hard time connecting with Talia, though he really doesn't get to spend as much time with her as I do since he's gone back to work.

162

I'm here at this hospital every single day.

Who am I fooling? There's a part of me that is afraid of getting attached to her. What if I have to say good-bye?

Talia is two weeks old . . . and they still have no answers. The most they know is that she has a very rare metabolic disorder that prevents her brain from telling her body what to do. She has no suck reflex, no gag reflex, and she can't regulate her own breathing.

I hate this roller coaster ride that has become my life. She's on life support . . . she's off it and starts breathing on her own . . . then she's on again because she turns blue . . .

"I . . . CAN'T . . . DO . . . THIS . . . GOD!" "THIS . . . IS . . . TOO . . . HARD!!"

My eyes are swollen from crying, I have a splitting headache from trying to make sense of these last couple weeks. Why is this happening? My heart hurts. While I'm grateful that I have a loving and supportive family, many times, I feel alone . . . and empty. I cannot do this anymore. I don't want to be me right now. I'm scared . . . I am so afraid of good byes . . . or maybe I'm just afraid of what I will feel after goodbye.

I'm afraid to have hope . . . I'm afraid to let go of hope. I'm. Just. So. Afraid.

This pain is unbearable. "God, what did I do to deserve this? If Talia was going to die, why wasn't she just another miscarriage? Am I being punished? Was I not a good enough mother for Ariana?"

God is not answering. I'm surprised at the guttural sounds that come out as I sob.

"God, I'm begging you to help me. Do you even exist? If you do, I don't know if you can even hear me. HELLLP ME! I . . . .CAN'T . . . .DO . . . .THIS. Please God . . . help me."

The only response I hear is silence.

Somewhere . . . somehow . . . in the midst of this silence, I begin to feel peace. This peace helps me to make it through another moment.

I begin to realize that I cannot control this journey. As the days progress, when I turn inward, I get an odd sense that I am not alone. That there is a presence that is with me, holding me when I can no longer hold myself together. Did it really take my brokenness to find that?

Our moments with Talia's little body come to an end. I don't know how to say goodbye . . . to Talia, to the nursing staff that became like family to us, to this hospital that became a second home.

I feel naked and vulnerable without the familiar routine that had become my life.

Two and a half weeks after Talia died, I hit a really low point. I don't want to be here anymore. I want to be out of my pain, and have no idea what could help. I decide to take a walk, and find myself sobbing for the entire four miles. I also realize I cannot stand looking at happy people right now.

A quarter mile from home, I notice an eighteen wheeler truck driving in my direction. With no thought of my husband or Ariana, I contemplate stepping off the curb. This would end my pain, I would be with Talia, and understand why life is the way it is.

Something stops me.

I walk home and decide to journal.

There are no words to be found. I am empty.

Silence.

A faint whisper inside my head breaks the silence.

"Mommy . . . "

I'm going crazy. I can't write that.

It persists, "Mommy . . . mommy . . . mommy . . . " I allow my pen to write "Mommy" . . . and then it is as if my pen has a life of its own, words flying out so quickly.

"Mommy, please know that I'm okay. There is so much love here, that I'm never alone. There is no suffering or heartache. You will see me again, although I'm not far from you now. Do you feel that peacefulness during times of great despair? That's us . . . taking care of you. Time is not relevant anymore, so don't think that it's going to be so long before we'll all be together again. I felt all the love from everyone at the hospital. Although I wasn't able to show it physically, I tried to give something back to each one of you. Remember the quiet times we had, and cherish those times alone.

At first I think I'm losing my mind. How could this message have come from Talia? Despite my doubt, my heart screams, "Believe it! Believe it!" Tears of happiness and gratitude replace any tears of sadness.

This message was just the beginning of a journey connected with the Other Side. This message evoked some big questions.

What really is "death"? What happens when you die? Is there really a non-physical realm called the "Other Side," and if so, how do you connect with it?

When you ask big questions of life, you get big answers. My answers brought me to a whole new world . . . and to my life's purpose.

I often say that my life was broken wide open during those 31 days that Talia was in the hospital. I understand on a soul level, that I did have an agreement to go through it all . . . so that I could understand death from a whole different perspective, become a Spirit Medium, and offer messages from heaven that would help so many others move through their pain.

No matter what you've gone through, there's a gift in your brokenness. I am proof of it. When Talia died, I truly thought I'd never be able to laugh or smile again.

You may want to ask, "How can I grow through this? What is this meant to teach me?" When you can embrace that life is happening "for" you, not "to" you, you can fully embrace the lessons and gift within each experience.

Here is one of my favorite pieces of writing that I hope will uplift your heart . . .

My dearest angels, what comfort would you like to give to anyone going through challenging times?

Give yourself permission to breathe. For your breath at this time is crucial to your healing. Each breath is an opportunity to bring new life into each cell of your body.

Give yourself permission to feel. The range of emotions that you will experience may feel as varied as the colors of the rainbow. You see the beauty of the rainbow, because each color is expressed. So, too, will you emerge through this, in fullness of strength, when you choose to experience each feeling that presents itself.

Give yourself permission to embrace any sadness or emptiness. While you already know this in the depths of your being, during the intensity of this time, you may forget that this period is temporary. Embrace these moments that you may call "darkness," for even in the spaces of darkness, there exists a ray of hope. It is there for all. Some will feel it, some will not.

Give yourself permission to feel our presence. We stand by you and hold you in our loving energy. We hear your cries, and always respond with love. You are never, ever alone.

Give yourself permission to understand that part of your pain may be from unresolved issues from the past. Welcome them, too, for healing. Old hurts, old patterns, or old guilt may resurface. Allow a full healing to occur . . . bringing love to all places within you that are holding on to these old energies.

Give yourself permission to trust. There may be questions that are left unanswered, many thoughts about your future that are uncertain. Please trust that you will be guided along every path, if you allow yourself. It is okay not to know all the answers in this moment.

Give yourself permission to simply be. Let go of the high expectations you may have held for yourself in the past. Forgive yourself for not feeling whole, for not "getting through this sooner," for not feeling happy. You are always whole, but you can certainly at times not feel it. Let that be Okay. When you don't know what to do with yourself, just breathe in the awareness of the present moment, and allow yourself to be there. There is nothing you have to do. Just let yourself be.

Breathe in our love for you. We are never far from you . . . just breathe.

The Womb of Darkness

I don't remember choosing to come here.

As I sit in the darkness, I feel my fear.

Unsure, disempowered, most definitely unaware . . .

Of the happier life I had before. The one with no cares.

I am blinded by this darkness. It makes no sense to fight. For the attempts have been futile And brought me no closer to the light.

I sit, I wait and I breathe.

I realize there is something that breathes me.

It tells me not to fear. For it has been with me through all time. I remember I'm not alone here.

About the Author

Sandy Alemian is a happiness coach, hypnotherapist, spirit medium, and the author two books, *Congratulations . . . It's an Angel* and the international best-seller *What was God Thinking?!* Through her written and spoken words, Sandy helps people awaken to their connection to the Infinite, so they can manifest a powerful life.

She is also the Founder and Chief Hugging Officer of YourDailyHug. com and the host of the widely popular podcast Healing Conversations . . . with Sandy Alemian." And because laughter holds healing power, Sandy has created an outrageous comedy stage hypnosis show. www.sandyalemian.com

Unwavering Strength Manifesto

Sandy Alemian

- When we sit with our brokenness, we have the potential to connect to something that can never be broken--the essence of our soul.

- We can all heal from tough times in our lives, but not everyone is aware of how to do this. Pain is inevitable. Suffering is optional.

- There is a part of us that is larger than whatever we are experiencing.

- Every experience offers an opportunity to help us to learn or grow. (Sometimes in moments of pain, it's so hard to understand how.)

- Whatever we experience here, we can create meaning from it by using it to help another person on their journey.

- Nothing can happen without it first being in our soul contract.

- Allowing ourselves to be vulnerable keeps us from having a hardened heart.

- Whenever we are upset, there is a powerful soul truth that can and will set us free.

- When we die, we'll fully remember that we truly are and always have been a part of the divine. And you don't have to die in order to remember that.

Team U.S. Our Ambassadors of Strength

Alice Therrault, Annie Spalding, Anya Sophia Mann, Bill King, Brian Bogardus, Brian Glidden, Cammie Ritchie, Corinne L. Casazza, Daniel Parmeggiani, Deb Oakland, Deb Scott, Emmanuel Dagher, Evelyn Roberts Brooks, Faith Poe, Irit Oz, Jeanne Henning, Jennifer Colford, John Burgos, Kellie Bishop, Lisa Barnett, Mark Lewis, Rebecca Field, Robert McDowell, Ron McElroy, Sandy Alemian, Sharon Campbell Raymont, Silke Nied, Dr. Terry Gordon, Tina Diez, Tracy Friesson, Wendy Knight Agard and Willie Tart.

Website: http://www.unwaveringstrength.com
Facebook: https://www.facebook.com/UnwaveringStrength
Twitter: https://twitter.com/UnwaveringStrgh

Music is the voice of the soul
the Music of Unwavering Strength

The following amazingly talented singers/songwriters have gifted you, the reader, with free downloads of their unique version of Unwavering Strength songs.

To get your free download please go to this page: http://unwavering-strength.com/songs/

"Unwavering Strength–Gerry's Song" is performed by Kristen Sharma and written by Jennifer Gibson

Kristen Sharma is a multiple award-winning entrepreneur in the healing arts industry, and everything she does carries the mission to heal and inspire the world. Kristen has been singing for over 30 years and is known for her rendition of the national anthem . . . and her pink boots. Her music and voice have been endorsed by Roger Love, America's #1 Voice Coach, and she has had the honor of singing for Michael Jordan, Anthony Robbins, Bob Proctor and many other notable leaders and hopes to sing at the United Nations one day soon. In 2012 she made it her personal mission to heal and inspire one billion people globally with her voice and music, as she believes music is the international language which can transform the heart and wrap the world in a blanket of love.

"Unwavering Strength–The Light and The Hope" is performed and written by Joe Merrick

Joe Merrick is an award winning singer/songwriter from Boston Massachusetts. He writes about the simple things in life as well as the complex. His latest accolades consist of opening up for The Steve Miller Band, and joining Carole King on stage, at a private party where he and band members played a set of American-themed songs and he later performed with King herself. For the past few months he's been singing for many major companies doing radio commercial spots. http://www.joemerrick.com.

"This is My Unwavering Strength"–vocals by Irit Oz, words and music by Ishay Oz Production: OH, Mark Kenoly & Gad Oz Background Vocals: Mark Kenoly, Ishay Oz & The OH Singing Group.
Special thanks to Mark Kenoly who dedicated days and nights to this production, demonstrating his love and unwavering strength (http://www.kingdomvoiceworship.com)

The power to choose is one of the strongest, most effective and impactful insights that a person can have. At OH, we promote awareness of the power of choice. We do this in many ways, including consulting projects with organizations, articles, children's books, and music. As we discovered over the last year , we were destined to do what we do today ever since we were children. We were always engaging people, and we always wanted to share our insights with others. We would like to spread love and compassion wherever we can, and we believe that real change comes when people understand the real strength that they have inside them. Each one of us can make a huge difference. We sometime feel that things are bigger than we are—that we can't really make a difference—but it's simply not true!!! This song is for everyone who has doubts, who feels insignificant. We have all been there, but we have chosen a new path, a new way. We call it, the OH WAY. In the OH way, you are very significant, you are the director of your life, and you have a limitless impact. We welcome everyone who wants to choose differently to join us. Now is our time to thrive.
More songs by OH can be found at: http://ozandhirshfeld.com/songs/.

These songs are a gift to you from these talented singer/songwriters. Each song was created with the intention to give you unwavering strength in difficult times. http://unwaveringstrength.com/songs/

Unwavering Strength, Volume 2

Deborah Oakland

Preview: Living in Courage

"Courage can take us to the deepest part of our soul where we find levels of reserve we did not know we had."
—Debra Oakland

In our second book *Unwavering Strength* you will meet Debra Oakland. Over a short six years Debra lost her 21-year-old son, her unborn baby girl in the 8th month of pregnancy, both brothers to AIDS and her father to prostate cancer. These events happened in quick succession with little time for emotional recovery.

Rather than succumb to despair and depression, Debra began her life-altering path and became a writer, courage advocate, and joy-full experiencer. Delving deep into her inner spirit Debra found herself wanting to share with others how she overcame some of life's biggest challenges. Debra will be sharing some of the *Unwavering Strength* tools she used to build a strong foundation of courage.

She learned it is possible to go through deep loss and live a happy life. Many of our darkest times can lead us into a beautiful place of light that illuminates our journey forward in unexpected ways. We can heal; grow stronger, wiser and more loving by embracing our inner power. As we share our personal stories of unwavering strength, what a difference we can all make in each other's lives. That's powerful!

Debra looks forward to sharing her "Living in Courage" message with you in our second book.

About the Author

Debra Oakland is the Founder of Living in Courage—A Spiritual Oasis For Overcoming Life's Biggest Challenges. Debra has been a contributor in several published books, online magazines and events, featured on many radio shows and is eagerly anticipating the release of her own book which has been a four year project.